SCREW EVERYONE

SLEEPING MY WAY TO MONOGAMY

OPHIRA EISENBERG

SEAL PRESS

SCREW EVERYONE
Sleeping My Way to Monogamy

Copyright © 2013 by Ophira Eisenberg

Published by
Seal Press
A Member of the Perseus Books Group
1700 Fourth Street
Berkeley, California

Library of Congress Cataloging-in-Publication Data

Eisenberg, Ophira, 1972-
  Screw everyone : sleeping my way to monogamy / By Ophira Eisenberg.
     pages cm
  ISBN 978-1-58005-439-3
  1. Eisenberg, Ophira, 1972- 2. Comedians—United States—Biography. 3.
Conduct of life—Humor. 4. Sex—Humor. I. Title.
  PN2287.E3955A3 2013
  792.702'8092—dc23
  [B]
                                              2012041690

10 9 8 7 6 5 4 3 2 1

Cover design by Elke Barter
Front cover photo © Jan Cobb Photography Ltd.
Interior design by Domini Dragoone
Printed in the United States of America
Distributed by Publishers Group West

DEDICATION

For Jonathan, who claims that counter to what
I wrote on page 221, he was not reluctant
about paying for the wine, whatsoever.

TABLE OF CONTENTS

Introduction 7

CHAPTER 1: First Kiss on My List................................. 13

CHAPTER 2: Expand Your Horizons............................. 25

CHAPTER 3: Nasty, Brutish, and Slutty.......................... 39

CHAPTER 4: Swan Dive 47

CHAPTER 5: Tommy, Can You Hear Me? 55

CHAPTER 6: Fijian Waters Run Deep 65

CHAPTER 7: The Whore of Fraser Island 77

CHAPTER 8: Hex an Ex... 91

CHAPTER 9: The Trouble with Fieldwork..................... 101

CHAPTER 10: Unsend.. 117

CHAPTER 11: Legally Blind.. 131

CHAPTER 12: The Nice Fetish... 141

CHAPTER 13: Rent a Wreck.. 151

CHAPTER 14: Screw No One... 165

CHAPTER 15: Goodnight, Charlie.................................... 185

CHAPTER 16: Endless Lasagna 199

CHAPTER 17: Turn Around, Bright Eyes 211

CHAPTER 18: The Last Comedienne.............................. 225

CHAPTER 19: Vanilla Mistress.. 241

CHAPTER 20: Know When to Fold 'Em........................... 261

CHAPTER 21: Unbridled... 273

Epilogue...283

EPIGRAPH

"My only regret in life is that I didn't drink enough Champagne."
—John Maynard Keynes

INTRODUCTION

The names of the men in this book have been changed because most of them are named Dave.

And there are a lot of names in this book. Then again, it *is* called *Screw Everyone*, so I'm delivering on that promise. You might wonder if the quantity of men indicates that I possess a special talent or I'm some sort of knockout. Au contraire, my friend. I'm not effortlessly pretty, but I do clean up well. My real gift is that I'm not fussy. If we were talking about food, I'd be considered "adventurous," in wine circles, "unpretentious," and in dating terms, "a slut." If there were such a thing as Lady Scouts, I would have easily earned the booty-call badge: an embroidered silhouette of a girl ordering two drinks at last call.

When most people think of a slut, they envision a woman who is a lost soul, wildly insecure, mentally unstable, and possibly dumb. Au contraire encore! I might not speak great French, but I am not dumb.

And I didn't set out to be a slut; frankly, I didn't even realize I *was* one. I just thought I was being nice.

Call me an enthusiastic consenter, or a fairly responsible hedonist, but sleeping around was often the by-product of getting what I wanted. I felt empowered going against the accepted "rules" of society by intentionally going home with a guy. They weren't just random guys. I *picked* them. That being said, I was an advocate of equal opportunity hook-ups, with everyone from jazz musicians to blind albinos.

Right from the start, I planned and strategized my potential romantic encounters like a veteran criminal. My quest in life went beyond wanting to "try anything"; I wanted to try *everything*. Sex and relationships became my drug of choice. What turned me on the most was the seduction, the thrill of trying to get someone to like me, and seeing how far I could take it. Rarely was it a problem to get the ball rolling; the issue was how to control it once it picked up speed. By my estimation, dating was 1 percent confidence and 99 percent troubleshooting.

And then there is the simple case of efficiency. Say what you will about going all the way on the first date, but if you want answers about compatibility faster than what Google can provide, it's the best way to go.

Plus, I like men. I never considered them "the enemy" or an unsolved mystery to be analyzed to death. I had too many other things to worry about. I didn't relate to any of the classic dating rules, either. If you believe you can master your romantic fate by playing games, like waiting three days to call someone or pretending to be busy on a Friday night when you're really just watching *Prime Suspect* with an overpriced bottle of Chardonnay, then fantastic. But I think the only person you're fooling is yourself. I'd rather slip into my favorite pair of jeans and head over to the local *Pig and Whistle* pub for a quick pick-me-up. Experience showed me that if there was anything I could count on in life, it was another beer and another boyfriend in my future.

After thirty years of intense study in Canada's school of relationships, I graduated by moving to New York City, which baffled me on every level. Much like affordable apartments, relationships were not easy to come by. I retaliated by boldly claiming that I didn't want to find "a relationship." I didn't believe there was such a thing as "the one." I wanted to have a good time and enjoy my freedom with guys I consciously didn't want to get to know. Underlying this was the fact that despite gender stereotypes, *I* was the one with an intense fear of settling down. I was sold on the idea that letting the same someone in, year after year, would stagnate my personality.

When men have this problem, it's called "commitment issues." When women have it, it's referred to as "hitting the jackpot." At least that's what most of the guys I dated thought.

As luck would have it, eventually I would be faced with a new challenge: I was introduced to someone who didn't respond to the brash and freewheeling character I'd invented for myself. Moreover, he wanted the real thing: marriage, commitment, stability, old-fashioned love—which, like a spray of DEET, repelled me and made me want to fly as far away as possible. Unfortunately, I'd already done that by moving to New York. So I stayed. And this is the story of how I discovered myself, conquered my fears, and even found the "real thing" through promiscuity. That may sound as backward as saying "cocaine saved my life!" but it's true. I traveled from flask to flask, futon to futon, gathering data, figuring one day I'd put it all together, and like a mad scientist, build my own perfect Boyfriend Bot. It's not the ideal plan for everyone, but I give it four gold stars.

I know I gave away the ending in the book's title, but I guarantee you that by the end you'll still be surprised that I got married, and a little that I'm still alive.

If you're wondering, *is this book for me?* Well, if you're the kind of reader who orders another round just to see if you can seal the deal with the depressed bass player because "Hey! I'm sad too! We have so much in common!" then the answer is yes. If, when you're on a first date, your guy finds an "old hit of acid" in his wallet, and you immediately agree to wash it down with an espresso, then not only is this book for you—it's also *about* you. And if you fell in love with your high school sweetheart and you're living "happily ever after" in a castle converted into condos, you need this book more than ever. It's how you'll deal with your next marriage.

If you're a guy whom I hooked up with in the past and you're now madly flipping through this book, wondering why you can't find your story, I need to tell you that unfortunately, not everyone made the cut. I'll let you know if I ever need to do callbacks.

Kidding aside, I'm very grateful for the men who populate the pages of this book. Not one of them could be classified as a true-blue asshole. They had their troubles, they had their habits, they had questionable haircuts, but with few exceptions, the guys I spent my bedtime with were totally worth it. Most were navigating through life as messily as I was, often unsure of what direction they were headed. So we slept together to see if that shed any light on the path. Some batteries just had a shorter lifespan than others.

These are the highlights of my relationship resume, from my newbie days as a tween to my efflorescence as a (mostly) willing bride-to-be. But before all those Daves, at the ripe age of eleven, I met my inspiration. A boy named Brad . . .

CHAPTER 1

FIRST KISS ON MY LIST

On the first day of seventh grade, I took my hair out of its two braids and wore it down for the very first time. This was junior high. Things were different. According to all the Judy Blume books I'd read, shit was about to get real.

On the second day, Brad Moore approached me after Mrs. Cairn's English class and asked me if I wanted to "go around." Brad Moore had curly brown hair, a freckled face, and a silly smile, but his most attractive quality was that he liked girls. While most other boys were still punching us in the arm and running away, squealing like preschoolers on a sugar high, Brad Moore was more likely to casually approach and tell you how pretty you looked in your rainbow suspenders. The guy knew how to work a homeroom.

I didn't know what "going around" meant; I pictured us arm in arm, promenading around the playground, while our classmates applauded. I had no idea if I even *liked* Brad Moore but figured the best way to find out was to say yes. My girlfriends deliberated and advised against it, claiming that going around was a slippery slope to getting knocked up. I was naive, but I wasn't dumb. I knew from observing my older siblings that he'd have to buy me *something* before he could do that. I think the real reason they were threatened by my budding romance with the class Don Juan was because I was the first girl in our group to get attention from a boy. I have no idea why he liked me. It certainly wasn't because I was the most attractive or most popular girl in our class, nor because I had the biggest video game console at home. Maybe it was because Brad Moore, even as a tween, had some primitive sense that I was the perfect girl for him: the kind who never says no.

In actuality, "going around" turned out to be a pretty lackluster affair. All we did was make dumb faces at each other in biology class and eat lunch at the same table. There was no applause or chance of a pregnancy scare. We didn't even hold hands. I couldn't understand what all the fuss was about. That is, until the night of the Halloween dance.

I went dressed as a sexy alien, in a purple and silver '60s mod dress I found at the Goodwill, my face covered with sparkles and my hair sprayed blue. He went as a punk rocker: green hair, fake tattoos, and a sleeveless jean jacket covered with safety pins—because *duh*, we all knew that large numbers of safety pins equaled punk rock. We slow danced to the last song of the night, Led Zeppelin's "Stairway to Heaven," edging closer and closer together until my lips were nearly pressed against his ear. I inhaled him deeply, and *whoa*, my nerves sparked like foil in a microwave. All of a sudden I understood every episode of *Dallas,* every Danielle Steel novel, every Tina Turner song. I hung on to him even tighter, as if it would ground me, but it only made the tingles intensify and multiply. To this day, the smell of tinted Halloween hairspray turns me on.

I ended up kissing Brad Moore, but that happened *after* we broke up. We terminated our short stint as classmates-with-slow-dancing-benefits via the 1980s equivalent of text messaging: passing notes. Based on the speed dating he did after our "breakup," he must have wanted first shot at all the seventh-grade girls before the other boys caught on that we weren't icky. I wasn't terribly heartbroken; I just wanted to climb more of that stairway to junior high heaven.

Three months later, I got my chance at Janet Vanderbroek's legendary Valentine's party. Packed in her wood-paneled basement that was decorated with rolls of red and pink streamers, we stood around nervously munching on bowls of potato chips and listening to Janet's recent purchase of ten cassette tapes for a penny from Columbia House, which included everything from Huey Lewis and The News to Quiet Riot. But the real centerpiece of the party was the cardboard Cupid hanging from the ceiling in the middle of the dance floor. Word quickly spread that the Cupid was ersatz mistletoe: If you ended up under it, you *had* to make out with the person you were dancing with. As the Orange Crush and root beer took hold, we loosened up, and Brad Moore, wearing his brand-new ripped jeans, made his way through the crowd and asked me to dance. Maybe he realized that playing the field wasn't all it was cracked up to be.

I don't remember what music was playing at that moment; it could have been a death metal band, for all I knew. All my attention was on our proximity to that cardboard Cupid. Working together like a Ouija planchette that magically slides to yes, we floated across the room until we were suddenly beneath it. Brad closed his eyes and leaned toward my face. *This is it!* I thought, nervous, but game. Our lips touched, and then his tongue shot into my mouth, wiggling around like a minnow caught on a fishing line. I quickly joined in with my own tongue. I may be a poor leader, but I'm an excellent follower and a quick study. It was more than childish kissing; we were really making out—just like in *Grease!* Looking back, I'd have to say that Brad Moore was a better kisser fresh out of the gate than many thirty-year-old men I've known. That's why I didn't bother changing his name. He should know that.

Everyone was gawking at us, some with disgust, others with envy, a few with a mixture of both, but I didn't care. It was better than eating bacon on Hanukkah morning. Days later, I could still feel the pressure of his lips, and for months afterward, I would replay that moment in my head every night before I went to sleep. The only stinger was that after our dance, Brad Moore asked every girl at the party to dance and kissed them all. Thank god I was first, and subsequently the only one who didn't come down with strep throat.

MY MOTHER DIDN'T raise me with fairy tales about some Prince Charming sweeping me off my feet and solving all my problems. "Wish on stars all you want," she would say, "but no one's listening except you." It sounds harsh, but what do you expect from a woman who grew up in World War II Holland? "Don't be picky," she warned, "it's not attractive." Looking back, I guess she was saying, "Be happy if someone likes you, and if it doesn't work out, try someone else." We weren't raised to be orchids, only blooming under perfect conditions. We were taught to thrive anywhere. Like a weed.

My parents met in Nijmegan, Holland, right after the German occupation. My dad was born in Israel (although back then it was sort-of Palestine) and was part of the Allied forces that liberated Holland from Germany. Eager to leave war-torn Holland behind, my mother agreed to the marriage and was pregnant at sixteen years old, living in the oh-so-peaceful land of sort-of Palestine. She raised my two older brothers there, but constantly complained that she'd only moved from one war zone to another. "I was sick of all the bombing, the guns all the time. I wanted a break," she would say, as if she were recalling a particularly rainy year. In 1957, they immigrated to Canada, the land of peace, snow, and opportunity. My dad started working as a Hebrew teacher, and then became the principal. Meanwhile, they had four more children. The only battles now took place in the living room, in the form of whining protests if we had to watch the news when Star Trek was on.

There are twenty-five years between my oldest brother and me. He and my next oldest brother already had wives and kids before I was even a trickle in the tap. I'm the youngest of six, and my mother had me late in her life. Back then if you were pregnant in your forties, you'd appear on *Ripley's Believe It or Not!*

As a family we joked around a lot. Sarcasm and teasing were the currency of affection. The dinner table was like an open mic, with whomever was oldest headlining. My brothers and sisters loved telling anyone who would listen how my mother cried and cried when she found out she was pregnant with me. They took to calling me "The Mistake." Once I asked my mom about this, and she told me not to worry—we were *all* mistakes.

If she could embrace her mistakes, even consider them happy errors, then the pressure was off me to make perfect choices. Maybe life wasn't so much about getting it right, as much as it was about rolling with the punches . . . or punch lines.

The year I was born, my father left education and bought three grocery stores. We lived in Calgary, Alberta, Canada, an affluent oil and cattle town near the Rocky Mountains. Calgary was about as ethnically diverse as a Joan Baez concert—or a Moby concert, or a Taylor Swift concert, depending on your age. The fact that we were Jewish, and a family of seven brunettes and one redhead, made us the most exotic household in the neighborhood, second only to the Chinese family that lived down the street. As a child, I hated how my name, Ophira, stuck out and no one even bothered to try to pronounce it properly. They called me Ophelia instead. Didn't that *Hamlet* character kill herself? Forget unrequited love; she probably did it because no one ever got her name right. My grade school teachers would scroll down the roll call list, study my pale face, light eyes, and suspiciously dark hair, and ask me if I was Black Irish, or maybe my parents were hippies? I'd tell them that my parents were twice their age, from Israel and Holland, and Ophira was an ancient Hebrew name; it just didn't catch on like Rachel or Sara. They'd nod and put a little red *x* beside my name. I was definitely a kid that needed to be watched. By singling me out as special, they created a standard that I'd strive to live up to.

Other than my odd name, which sounded more like a brand of contact lens solution than something you'd call a little girl, I had something else that distinguished me as "unusual" among my peers. At eight years old, I survived a terrible car crash that left me with a scarred body and a sense of urgency. Perhaps this is why I raced faster than my friends to conquer life's benchmarks as soon as possible.

While driving home after a day spent swimming at the Jewish Community Center, we were rammed into by a guy who'd run a red light. Unconscious and in critical condition, I was rushed into emergency surgery with a punctured lung and liver, a ruptured spleen, a head wound, broken ribs, and a medley of other broken bones. The doctors told my father I had a 50/50 chance of making it. Upon hearing this, I'm told, a gigantic smile spread across his face, and he started marching up and down the hospital halls, yelling, "Did you hear that? Fifty percent! She's going to live! Fifty percent! She is going to make it!"

I like to think that I heard him.

Thankfully he was right. Not only did I make it, I walked out fully intact, with a souvenir scar in the shape of a slightly off-kilter Y that runs the length of my torso, from breastbone to pelvic bone, and across my midsection, from belly button to my right side. It's big, and it looks pretty cool.

In gym class, if we had to change, I could feel girls staring at my stomach. They had a right to be curious—I would have been too. As budding young women, we were fixated on one another's bodies. Some of us were growing hips, some breasts, some crazy body hair, while others—i.e., me—had a little of each, plus a big pinkish scar. As puberty fully took hold, I, too, became self-conscious, worried that guys would freak out if they saw it (as it turns out, I should have been more concerned about the guys who would be really *into it*. *Blech.*).

After another uncomfortable health class filled with stifled laughter and awkward fidgeting over details about our impending hormonal future, I was walking home with my friends Tania and Megan, discussing important stuff—namely, who in our class would most likely become a stripper (for the record, it was a girl named Becca Dickerson). That's when it hit me. I couldn't even screw up my life and fall back on topless waitressing or stripping like other girls could. Due to my scar, I wasn't even in the running. It was so unfair! What strange XXX club would have a girl taking off her clothes to reveal a large operation scar? Maybe a fetish club, but I didn't know about those—yet (my future policy to never leave an unmarked basement door unopened would eventually lead me to one). I had no choice but to get my shit together.

As kids, it hadn't occurred to us that tragedies could happen to anyone we knew, let alone at our age. The fact that it happened to me meant that I was treated differently, and consequently I thought differently. After the accident, I grappled with the idea that random acts could throw everything off course. Bad things happened. Life wasn't going to take care of me, and I had to agree with my mother that waiting for things to happen organically was an utter waste of precious time. You want a cupcake? Go buy one. They only have lime ones left? Guess what your new favorite flavor is. As I got older, this translated to: If I wanted a job, apply! A boyfriend? Ask him out! To lose my virginity? Make it happen! To fall in love? Okay, that was a little more difficult, but having a job, a boyfriend, and some sexual experience would give me a running start.

MY FATHER DIED the summer before I entered high school, and our family broke into fragments. At almost sixty years old, my mother had to go to work and manage the grocery stores. Within a year, she was doing things I'd never seen her do before: going out dancing, dating, having fun. The last of my siblings moved out, and for the first time the household was just two people: me and my mom. Even though it was a period of great transition, we relished the space and freedom it gave us. All of a sudden, the house had too many couches to lie on, too many remotes to control, too much silence. My mother relaxed the rules and my curfews in exchange for me letting her date without interference. I could basically do whatever I wanted, with virtually no one to answer to, as long as I kept up with my responsibilities. And trust me, I took advantage of it. It *is* possible to keep your grades up AND drop acid.

Luckily Calgary was a nice, safe place—it was like the walls were made of soft sponges. You had to work really hard to get in trouble. The mere fact that I was considered one of the primary instigators among my friends was a sign of how nonthreatening the place was. I was the one with all the ideas, and I'd drag friends through the "bad" parts of town (indicated by an overflowing garbage can) and ask derelicts if I could buy their hash. We'd layer our faces with makeup and tell doormen that not only were we eighteen, but we'd also been personally invited to the nightclub by the owner. Rarely did anyone question or refuse us. It was a talent I'd parlay into every aspect of my later life: approach with confidence, know what you want, and just tell them. I've found that it works very well with men, but not with immigration officers or tax auditors.

Despite my late-night shenanigans, I still managed to make it to school, perform reasonably well, and show up for my shifts at the grocery store.

I liked having a job. It gave me pocket money to pay for cover charges and Bartles & Jaymes wine coolers. My mother increased my work tasks incrementally, and soon I was even doing the ordering, everything from groceries to hardware to magazines. Never was a teenager more in tune with news, celebrity gossip, trendy fashions, and, of course, men's sexual fantasies. That's right, I wouldn't just sort and restock all those magazines when they came in; I'd *read* them all—or at least check out the pictures.

In retrospect, what appeared in the shiny pages of the men's magazines we placed on the upper shelf of the magazine rack—like *Bear, Playboy,* and *Swank*—was pretty tame by today's standards. I think I've seen more hardcore porn on Bravo lately. But if my memory serves me right, the material wasn't *that* degrading. I'm sure Naomi

Wolfe would like to kill me, because yes, the women were being objectified, but I didn't perceive it that way. What I saw was a bunch of tarted-up women not so much exploited as exploiting a situation to their advantage.

The story spreads were my favorite: five pages of glammed-up women applying for jobs as secretaries, or being coached on the tennis court. They were both hilarious and fascinating. Everyone started out so nice and professional looking, in polyester blouses with floppy bows or proper white tennis dresses, always paired with Lucite stilettos (see-through goes with everything), but within one panel all the clothes would be off. Good storytelling starts in the action. By panel four, not only did they score the job or improve their swing, but they looked like they were having a damn good time doing it. Sure, maybe my perspective was a bit skewed, but I preferred the dynamics of these scenes over the more passive ideal of timid girls pining in the wings, hoping to get asked to the dance, and scoring poorly on *Cosmo* quizzes. I didn't have the luxury to wait around hoping for some mythical right time or right person to appear, like some precious orchid waiting for the right conditions of light and water to blossom and grow. I needed to be like a weed, and thrive *now*. Brad Moore had the right idea. I, too, wanted to get out there and kiss, "go around," and eventually screw whomever I desired, maybe *everyone* I desired. Who cared if I made mistakes? I'd figure it out, with or without a cardboard Cupid to guide me.

CHAPTER 2

EXPAND YOUR HORIZONS

My first couple of experiences with sex didn't exactly go as planned. Then again, neither did the next forty. When I hear about women who have tidy, pretty, lingerie-infused sexual encounters, all I think is, *Where's the part where you break your toe and have to mop up?* Some women's torrid love affairs belong in movies with James Bond. Others of us, with Will Ferrell.

At the beginning of August, I began counting down the days to the start of high school. I couldn't wait to walk down the hallways in slow motion with my posse, like in a John Hughes movie, and I didn't even have that many friends. It was the *potential* that fueled my enthusiasm. Take this entry from my high school diary, dated September 1: "I know this year is going to be amazing. I want an amazing life, full of the most wonderful times, friends, boyfriends, laughs and tears, boyfriends, and for the upcoming years to be the best years EVER!"

Yes, I wrote *boyfriends* and *amazing* twice.

Western Canada High was not only the biggest high school in Calgary but also the coolest, situated in the heart of the city and surrounded by cute dress shops, restaurants, and cafés. Taking the public bus there every morning made me feel so grown-up—like I was going to my sexy job at a detective agency rather than to a dry biology class taught by a teacher so boring that the chapter on reproductive organs wasn't even funny. My mother gave me fifty dollars for first-day-of-school clothes. My challenge: find an outfit that would communicate a unique sense of style that everyone wanted to copy but couldn't, no matter how hard they tried. I'd be untouchable. The answer was Le Chateau, a retail chain that sold cheap, trendy clothing to high school girls whose parents had given them fifty dollars. It was also where all my friends shopped. Somehow we believed that the mass-produced lacey tops and identical jewel-toned felt berets we wore marked us as individuals. Lucky for me, I was able to set myself apart by being one of the few who looked good in mustard.

Although the standard cliques were well represented at our school—jocks, headbangers, stoners, nerds—the student body was essentially divided into two groups: the smart people and the rest of us. The smart people were enrolled in this Geneva-based International Baccalaureate Program, or the IB Program. Fortunately for them, it was before irritable bowel syndrome was a household name. This education program offered advanced classes for the more gifted students, ensuring them acceptance into prestigious colleges, and all but guaranteeing them plum careers at companies like AIG, Lehman Brothers,

Pfizer, and other top-notch corporate empires. The rest of us would have to settle for a shitty education at a mediocre college and a future working at some podunk company where our uncle knew the manager.

The clincher was that my application for the IB Program was rejected. During my interview with the Ministry of Swiss Intelligence, or whatever they called themselves, they claimed that the amount of time I spent in ballet classes would distract me from my studies. To which I blurted, "Listen, I'm a terrible dancer, not very flexible, and I can barely keep my balance in a double pirouette!" In retrospect, pleading mediocrity probably wasn't the best strategy, but I accepted my fate. It was just as well. I didn't fit their profile. I had decent grades but no specific plans to make anything of myself. This is not to say I didn't have ambition—my focus was deeper. Per my journal, I had goals. Secure a boyfriend. Spiral-perm my hair. Lose my virginity. Probably in reverse order.

As with most high schools, the popular students at mine were the athletic rich kids, and I can tell you, I was neither of those things. It didn't matter. I had no interest in being popular. I related more to the math whizzes, chemistry lab nuts, and drama geeks anyway. Ferris Bueller was my social role model, and I aspired to be a friend to all, without having to conform to any one clique. The ultimate self-assured outsider. Who knew this would prepare me for the life of a stand-up comic?

Also, I wanted to get my virginity *over with*, lose the new-car smell of my adolescence, shower, and start living *real* life. I worshipped my older sister, who moved back home after a fight with her boyfriend when she was twenty-seven. The fight was so monumental that he apologized for it by buying her a nose job, a toy poodle, and a massive diamond ring. She accepted all the gifts but wasn't interested in moving back in with him right away. I looked up to her so much, it surprised me that we were the same height. Even though we lived under the same roof, she existed in an alternate universe, one in which a looping conveyer belt ferried her daily from her bed, to her makeup vanity, through her extensive closet, then out the other side bedecked in spandex and sequins, where she'd be whooshed out the front door to a vast network of parties and bars—then back again for another round. She spoke to me like a fortuneteller, warning me of my future. It didn't look promising. Before I'd even swallowed one drop of alcohol, she predicted that vodka would make me argue with my boyfriend (she was right), and that I'd also suffer a falling out when in the presence of Jose Cuervo and Captain Morgan. She promised me that losing my virginity would not be the beautiful and romantic experience movies made it out to be. Instead, it would be more akin to how English philosopher Thomas Hobbes described the life of man in his natural state: nasty, brutish, and short. "Don't waste it on someone special that you really love," she advised. "Just get it over with so you can move on to better sex."

The realization that I had control over how and when I lost my virginity empowered me. If my thighs were actually going to balloon out as much as my sister said they would over the next ten years, I needed to get sexually proactive.

Up to that point, I'd done my fair share of kissing, and even skipped past second base with a Latino guy I met at a teenage nightclub called The Flipside. This was one of those all-ages dance clubs where fourteen- and fifteen-year-old kids would go to bop around to Madonna, Depeche Mode, and The Cure while downing five-dollar sodas.

Guys we didn't know would ask us to dance, including this Latino kid who resembled my music idol, Prince. While Echo and the Bunnymen's "Lips Like Sugar" segued into Prince's "The Beautiful Ones," he held me close, reached under my denim pencil skirt, and proceeded to finger me. I was fascinated that I could get to third base while standing vertically on a dance floor. It was more shocking than titillating, but it was progress. I applauded his dexterity. His hand snaked in there like an electrician finding a light switch in the dark. While he continued, my mind wandered to what would happen next. Would I have a boyfriend at a different high school? It had never occurred to me to look beyond the blue-lockered confines of our hallways. Would I go to two proms? I hoped he was from one of those bad schools in the Northwest.

The song ended, and Boy George's "Do You Really Want to Hurt Me" came on next. Not knowing what to do or say, I thanked him and dashed away to regale my friends with the details of my dance-floor diddle. They were in awe and asked me to point out the handy bandit, hoping he'd ask them to dance next. I looked around but my Latino lover had disappeared into the throng of dancing teenagers, perhaps to find a bathroom to wash his hands. We didn't exchange numbers, and after thinking about that finger-bang moment over and over again for a couple of days, I learned that The Flipside had been shut down because some kids had smuggled in shampoo bottles filled with alcohol. We'd hit the end of an era before it had even gained traction and settled back into our routine of scanning the gymnasium's bleachers for potential suitors.

Most of my friends were appalled that I wanted to "get rid of" my virginity as soon as I could, as if I were talking about back acne or a sticker collection. To them, casting off my chastity so flagrantly sounded sinful and slutty. They stressed that popping your cherry with just anyone would be yucky and depressing and I'd regret it forever. My friend Cheryl was the only one who agreed with me. She was in the IB Program. She was also considered one of the prettiest girls in our high school and was a math and science wizard. Her logical brain saw the strengths of my theory. Either that or she was an enabler. It didn't matter—Cheryl and I instantly became inseparable.

One Saturday afternoon, we were hanging out in Cheryl's basement doing what we always did: listening to Prince while working on our Lotus 123 spreadsheet titled "Potent.wk1" ("potentials" being too long for the file name conventions of that era). We used it to rate guys on their looks, personality (which we called the "nice quotient"), and type of car they drove, and then converted these stats into a pie chart so we could see whose slice came up the biggest. I suggested that we should try losing our virginity on the same night—not to the same guy, of course, or in any scenario worthy of pay-per-view programming, but more as an intellectual data-gathering experiment. Cheryl agreed this was an excellent plan. But where could we set up our lab? It clearly had to be somewhere away from our parents, school, and prissy friends. And where would we find these lab-rat guys to begin with? While our game of sexual Sudoku was missing a few numbers, we could still prepare for it, so we came up with a code phrase to signal each other if the moment was right: "Expand your horizons." Brilliant.

To set the plan in motion, we met at Cheryl's locker every lunch hour, located on the floor that was allocated to the IB Program, and ate our sandwiches while a bunch of the gifted and talented boys buzzed around us. What I lacked in blonde hair and high school ambition, I made up for in my ability to do silly impressions—especially of my family. I soon became known as "Cheryl's jokey friend Ophira." Did this win me dates? Not exactly, but at least they knew my name.

Among this small swarm of IB boys were a pair of twins named Jake and Matt. While they weren't lab-trial quality, they had very high nice-quotients and were constantly trying to impress Cheryl. One day, they mentioned that they played in a rock band with two other guys. *A rock band?!* Cheryl and I were instantly intrigued. When could we see their band in action? we asked, and who *were* these other members? Jake told us (Or was it Matt? Who could tell.) that the lead singer and bassist ate their lunch in the cafeteria. No wonder we'd never met them! Since we brought our own bag lunch, we rarely ventured into the high school equivalent of a mess hall. It was time for a field trip. Cheryl and I grabbed our notebooks, reteased our bangs, and descended down to the lunchroom. Here, Jake and Matt motioned toward a couple of unoccupied gray enamel stools attached to the folding cafeteria table that the band claimed as their own.

Like any teenage girl worthy of her Jordache skinny jeans, I instantly fell for Robby, the band's lead singer. He had dark-brown hair that he gelled out into a spiky halo like The Cure's Robert Smith—just a little shorter in the front to conform to the grooming code of the chain restaurant he worked at on weekends. The band, we learned, played U2 covers exclusively and called itself "B4"—a name that Robby had come up with, which in my notebook meant he was a borderline genius. I was smitten. Unfortunately for me, Cheryl had a crush on him too, which made mine all the more acute because Cheryl's was reciprocated.

This left me with Robby's dorky best friend, Cameron.

Tall and lanky, with dirty-blond hair that was more Robert Plant than Robert Smith, Cameron was the bass player for B4. He was nerdy. He was smart. But he liked me, and I figured anyone in the band was close enough. It bothered me that he was so quiet, but it would later turn out to be a valuable trait.

The first time I saw B4 play live was at a house party—a house party that *I'd* booked them for. It was spring, and my mother decided she needed a break from working long days at the grocery story and dealing with her two sour teenagers—me and my eighteen-year-old brother, the last of the six children she'd raised. Who could blame her? She booked herself a ten-day trip to visit her family in Holland. My older sister went on a vacation to Mazatlán with her on-and-off-again diamond-nose job-poodle-buying boyfriend, leaving my brother and me alone for half a month. The timing couldn't have been better. I was going to do the one thing that I'd promised my mother I would never ever do: throw a party. A big one. In addition to recruiting B4 to play, I also planned to serve alcohol—courtesy of my brother. Before I had the nerve to ask him (I'd even rehearsed my plea), he'd already taken it upon himself to bring home a case of beer and a case of wine coolers—the latter for my inner circle of girlfriends. He was a good brother. He was also a *stoned* brother, and he figured that the more drunk we were, the less we'd notice him hot-knifing hash on the kitchen stove. We had booze, a band, and a basement. It was more than any fifteen-year-old could ask for.

I loved the idea of breaking the rules, and I say "idea" because by the morning of the party I was a nervous wreck, scared stiff that nobody would come, and if they did, that something would get damaged, someone would spray-paint our lawn, or one of my drunk girlfriends would throw up under a couch cushion. I went nuts, preparing the house as if I were expecting an army of toddlers to arrive. I removed all the vases, taped up sharp corners, and moved out of harm's way anything that could be crushed, broken, or vomited on. It was a smart move because at seven o'clock the entire school showed up. Instead of losing myself in the revelry, I ran around policing different rooms to make sure no one had too much fun. I actually started to wish my mother were there. She could have controlled the party while I rebelled against her, and we'd both relax.

A few hours later, when B4 plugged in their instruments to tune them, it hit me that this was one hell of a good party and I should try to enjoy myself. They started their set with U2's hit of the year, "With or Without You." Cheryl and I leaned against the basement support beam and swayed to the music, sipping our fizzy coolers. I was mesmerized by Robby's singing but made sure to smile a lot at Cameron. When the set ended, as a treat I passed around a bottle of Schnapps

I'd found in my mom's liquor cabinet. Judging by the layer of dust on the label, it had probably been sitting there since the first Star Wars movie came out in theaters. After sharing a swig with Cameron, I led him into the "makeout room"—my mother's sewing room—where we necked and dry humped in between quilt squares and sprigs of crinoline from my ballet costumes. We were both such novices, our groping ended up being too licky and fast paced. Occasionally our teeth would collide. At the end of the night when I puked, it was from the combination of worry, wine coolers, and a dash of melon Schnapps. Cameron biked home on his beat-up ten-speed, and I scrubbed the house and my mouth for two days. It was a near-perfect teenage evening.

A month later, my friend Karen announced that her parents were going out of town, and *she* also wanted to throw a party and have B4 play at it. Clearly, I had set a new standard. No longer was it acceptable to play mix tapes on your ghetto blaster. That was so 1987.

The boys took the gig, and I helped them set up their amps, pedals, and cables on the orange shag carpet of Karen's basement. While Cameron turned on his amp and checked his pedals, I daydreamed about my future as the band's tour manager, of how I'd walk around, yapping orders in a sleek-fitting pinstripe suit. I'd still be with Cameron but sleeping with Robby on the sly. This would go on for years. It was the closest I'd ever come to having career goals. No wonder I didn't get into the IB Program. They didn't offer a course called "Infidelity and Cover Band Management."

Cheryl had to study for a brain biology test or something, so I'd have to sway to the band on my own. On their set break, Cameron grabbed my hand and pulled me into the make-out room. In Karen's house, it was the furnace room. Only Freddy Krueger would find it romantic, but it was all we had to work with. After a lot of fevered making out, Cameron told me that he wanted to go down on me for the first time. My eyes lit up. Finally! Yes! I was on track, taking steps toward the ultimate objective. I was positively giddy as he slipped off my ruffled skirt and black Jockey-for-Her underwear, tossing them haphazardly into the abyss of the boiler room. I lay back on the cement floor as he dove in between my thighs. I wasn't sure what to expect, but what I felt was . . . light punching, like he was cramming his face into me. After about a minute of that I felt something wet, and then nothing. I opened my eyes and half sat up. There was Cameron, looking back at me, his head framed by the V of my legs, his face covered in blood.

I know exactly what this sounds like—but trust me, it wasn't that. If I had *that* story, I'd surely tell it. Apparently some unlucky combination of Cameron's excitement, the dry furnace air, and his amateur technique had caused his nose to bleed. I grabbed his T-shirt and tried to sop up as much blood as I could, but it was gushing uncontrollably.

"We need to get some ice or a towel or something," I said.

"We need to get Robby!" he whimpered.

"Wait!" I yelled, but before I could find my skirt or my underwear, a sliver of light fell on my thighs. Robby had slipped in and was now staring at me, my half-naked body in plain view.

I watched Robby's eyes move from Cameron's face to my thighs and then dart back to Cameron's face. Searching for a way to conceal my embarrassment, I finally looked Robby square in the face and said, "What? You've never seen this before?" As if his lack of experience, not my state of bloodied nudity, was the humiliation here. As if I were saying, "That's right, this shit happens all the time when you hang out with Ophira Eisenberg!" I followed it up with a frantic plea for him to fetch some ice and a towel. Robby, wide-eyed, nodded and ran off. With him gone, I scrambled around the floor and finally located my skirt; my underwear was never to be seen again. Abandoning the still-bleeding Cameron, I rushed out and found Karen, the hostess. I held her by her boney shoulders and backed her into the yellow guest bathroom. "What have you heard?" I demanded.

"Just that Cameron got a nosebleed but it's not nothing that Robby's never seen before." All those double negatives added up to a major positive, and I fell in love with Robby even more for keeping his highly kissable mouth shut. I told Karen I needed a minute and shoved her out of the bathroom. Underwearless with specks of dried blood on my thighs, I adjusted my skirt to conceal all the evidence and returned to the party as if nothing were amiss. This wasn't exactly the unique sense of style I'd set out to cultivate, but I felt pretty confident no one would be able to copy it. It was truly one of a kind.

The boys played their final set, and Cameron wouldn't look at me. This would never be an amusing story we'd tell our children. After that night, we drifted apart. We didn't officially break up as much as we petered out. It was a mutually agreed-upon avoidance, and because he didn't talk that much, I stopped waiting for him to deal with me directly and switched my attention to another group of guys. I'm pretty sure the story of his bloody face and my naked ass never ran through the gossip mill, for which I will always credit Robby and Cameron's discretion. I'm still waiting for someone to knock on my door holding a Ziploc bag containing a dusty pair of black Jockey-for-Her underwear excavated from a boiler room and ask me to explain. No, I got off easy with not much more than a shared secret and some missing panties, even if my virginity was still intact. Back to the Lotus spreadsheet to see what piece of pie would eat me next.

CHAPTER 3

NASTY, BRUTISH, AND SLUTTY

Cheryl and I thought Banff might be the perfect place for us to "expand our horizons." A cute ski town nestled in the Rocky Mountains, Banff attracted every good-looking human in the area for spring skiing, drinking, and hooking up. Getting permission from our parents was barely an issue. Cheryl and I both had working moms, absent fathers, and good grades, a harmonious combination as long as you returned home with washed hair and all your fingers.

We made certain we drove the speed limit, although with every click of the odometer we felt more and more like we were already breaking the law by heading to an unchaperoned weekend in Banff. If I'd known earlier that a 90 percent grade in physics signified that you were responsible, I would have studied harder, sooner. Cheryl managed to borrow her mother's car for the two-hour drive. I "borrowed" my mother's credit card and reserved a room at a cheap motel. I remember calling out to my mom from the kitchen while rifling through her purse, "Mom, I'm going to Banff for the weekend with Cheryl! Be back on Sunday!" and hearing, "Okay, be careful!" from the laundry room. At the time, that was considered solid parenting. Then again, this was long before you had to show an ID to buy cold medicine.

Green Mountain Lodge sounded a lot nicer than it was. I've never stayed in a more pathetic place. It hung on to its two-star rating by a fraying set of bed sheets, awarded by a local paper called *Pioneers Weekly*. It was the kind of place you stayed at if you were planning a murder, running from a killer, or generally second-guessing every decision you'd ever made in life. The bedspread had burn holes, and the carpet was an indistinguishable gray/brown/green color, the same fiber you'd find in a dog kennel. The only decor in our room was a watercolor of two chipmunks fighting over a nut and a placard titled EMERGENCY EVACUATION INSTRUCTIONS. Ultimately, all that mattered was that we had our very own crash pad in a town filled with ripped boys waiting to fall prey to our naive charm. Hopefully, we wouldn't get carded.

As soon as our duffel bags hit the floor, we faced our first major challenge: transforming ourselves into college students who passed for the legal drinking age. With the help of Bonne Bell makeup, sparkly tops, miniskirts, and high heels, we looked more like two girls trying too hard to look eighteen than two girls who were actually eighteen, which was enough to get us in anywhere.

Tentative in our heels, we wobbled down the main strip of bars, every one of them embracing a cabin or moose theme. We'd made it one block when a couple of guys called out from the window of a bar, beckoning us to join them. It seemed like a perfectly valid invitation to us, even if they were drunken strangers. They offered to buy us a beer, and we gave them our fake names, ones we'd agreed upon earlier. By combining our respective middle names with our moms' maiden names, Cheryl became Lynn Collingwood and I was now Ms. Jasmin van Brunswick. *My fake name sounded even faker than my real name.* We giggled and told them that we worked as chemistry and biology lab technicians. It was sort of true; Cheryl and I had after-school jobs setting up the labs for experiments and exams. We were paid $3.25 an hour, which was pretty much why we were staying at the Green Mountain Kennel. They claimed to be air force pilots. It was consistent with how they looked; they were both physically fit, with bulging biceps and tight, short haircuts. Cheryl—I mean Lynn—whispered to me, "You know what that means—they're clean!" Top Gun! That Cheryl-Lynn was always thinking! They didn't seem to have any interest in investigating whether or not we fit our story. Lynn and Jasmin, a couple of eighteen-year-old lab technicians, was good enough for them.

The brunette was cuter, but the strawberry blond, although goofier, kept the conversation rolling. After two rounds of drinks, they shifted gears and invited us back to their hotel for "last call." We didn't even know what that meant. Their hotel, it turned out, was conveniently located across the street from ours, although it ranked about forty stars higher. The room was nice, but it was clear that they'd been up to some serious partying in it. The room was littered with beer cans, take-out food containers, and towels. I shoved aside a small mountain of crumpled white towels to sit down while the goofy one mixed up something called a Purple Jesus, a classy drink made from grape juice and pure grain alcohol. No cocktail should ever be purple.

Before I could finish mine—and I was trying—Cheryl was already making out with Maverick on the balcony. Goose grabbed my arm and pulled me over to the other side of the room. I caught Cheryl's half-opened eye and mouthed, "Expand your horizons?" She nodded slowly and gave me the thumbs-up. Goose tugged at my bra strap and dragged me into the bathroom.

After some sloppy kissing, the ritual of clothing removal began. He ripped off his T-shirt as if to say, "Here's what we're doing—look, I'll go first!" I hated taking off my shirt, only because it meant explaining the whole scar on the stomach thing. I hadn't yet prepared the thirty-second elevator pitch version of it, so instead I went back to kissing him. He stopped me a couple of minutes later and asked, "Can I take off your shirt?" (Canadians—we're so polite!) For the first time that night, I felt waves of panic. I knew where we were headed. I was about to lose my virginity. I replied "yes," but I didn't recognize the voice that said it. He started working fast, furiously kissing me on the neck and tugging on zippers. It took a while, as there were a lot of them, plus snaps and grommets—it was the fashion of the time. Next I was hoisted onto the bathroom counter, in between the sink and the travel shampoos. There was no mention of the scar; it was like he didn't see it. Cool. He was about to remove my underwear (I'd graduated from Jockey-for-Her to Elita) when I stopped the action and did the one thing that still makes me proud: I asked him to put on a condom. He, of course, didn't have one handy. Being the sophisticated, mature woman I was pretending to be, I fished the one I'd gotten from sex education class out of my purse, and much to his chagrin, handed it to him. That was it. We were officially about to "do it."

To say it was disappointing is an understatement. Losing my virginity was about as exciting as going around. Even though I was losing it to an older guy in an unconventional setting, the act itself fit my older sister's prediction: two minutes long and kind of annoying. The only thing she missed was the part where I got a free shower cap at the end of it. I hoped she was right about sex getting better the more you did it. If not, those porn stars in *Swank* should be given acting awards. Despite my months of imagining what it would feel like, I was glad that it didn't hurt, but other than the sensation of two bodies rhythmically slapping against each other, I didn't feel much of anything. Emotionally, it was a different story. My nonchalance turned into fear and embarrassment the moment he pulled out and began peeling off the condom. I became anxious about cleaning myself up, convinced that some renegade sperm was trying to crawl into my vagina.

He left the bathroom and I looked in the mirror. I did lose my virginity, right? Should I ask him? How would that go? *We did that, right? So it's done. Right? I'm good? Cool. Thanks.*

Goose returned with a couple of pillows, a sheet, and a blanket and tossed them on the floor. I guess it would be awkward if we slept in the double bed beside our friends. We exchanged quick smiles as he smoothed out the sheet.

"You can have the pillow," he said.

So that's what you have to do to get the pillow.

I wanted to run out and share notes with Cheryl, but at the same time, I didn't want to interrupt her "expanding horizons," so I fell asleep, curled up on our bathroom-floor bed with Goose beside me. In a twisted way, it was kind of sweet.

He asked, "Are you sure you're eighteen, Jasmin van Brunswick?"

"Yup" was the last thing I said before we passed out.

EARLY THE NEXT morning, I woke up to Maverick trying to step over us, asking if he could use the bathroom. *You mean the deflower room?* I thought, suddenly feeling self-conscious in the morning glare of the previous night's adventure. It didn't help that I was mildly hungover, or maybe still drunk. Cheryl stood near the door, already dressed, waiting for me so we could leave. There was an air of uneasiness among the four of us. I asked Goose if they wanted to grab some breakfast, thinking maybe if we all sat down and ate pancakes, things would feel a little more normal and familiar, but he said they had some very special training to get to ASAP, and we had to leave. In wrinkled miniskirts and smudged makeup, Cheryl and I took our very short walk of shame across the street to our shitbag hotel. I was ready to burst.

Finally I blurted, "So . . . how was 'expanding your horizons?!'"

"What do you mean?" she asked defensively. "I didn't 'expand my horizons.' We just made out a lot."

Alarm bells began to sound in my head, heart, and gut.

"What? I thought you were into it! You said yes when I said the code phrase!"

"No! I thought you were asking if I was okay. I wasn't really into that guy. Plus, I figured you wouldn't go all the way with a strange man in a hotel *bathroom!*"

Wow. She had higher standards for me than I did.

Little did I know this was the beginning of a pattern.

After the shock subsided, it occurred to me that the deed was done, with or without all pact participants. I had set out to lose my virginity and I'd done it. Check! I should have felt proud, changed, matured, and ready for the next step, but instead I felt a little confused, and a little lonely. Maybe that was growing up. From the point of view of a chemistry lab technician, the results of my popped cherry were inconclusive, but I was eager to do more research. Cheryl didn't say much more about it, other than she felt a little jealous, and I didn't push the conversation out of fear of adding to the distance the night had wedged between us. That was it. Time to get coffee and drive back into our respective horizons.

Cheryl and I returned to well-worn topics of future hair plans and final exams, and with no one to review my experiment with, I took a renewed interest in the chapter on reproduction in my biology text-book. But as my 90 percent in physics would tell you, bodies in motion stay in motion. And I was one of those bodies.

CHAPTER 4

SWAN DIVE

My mother still thinks that she caught me losing my virginity, but what could I say? "Don't worry, Mom, I lost it months ago to a fake air force pilot on a hotel bathroom counter." So I let her believe Tommy was my first.

Tommy was my high school sweetheart, although nothing about him was sweet. No parent, after meeting Tommy, would say, "What a delight! Now that boy is marriage material." Considering his two favorite bands were Black Flag and The Dayglo Abortions, I was surprised we met at a Midnight Oil concert. It must have seemed like easy listening to him. Australia fever had hit America (and therefore Canada), thanks to Paul Hogan's Crocodile Dundee empire, and my friend Kelly had scored us two tickets to see the Oils live. I carefully picked out a black-and-white striped half-top for the event and paired it with black jeans and Doc Martens: feminine yet edgy.

By sheer luck, our high school's biggest heartthrob, Sven, was right behind us at the concert. Sven was a true Sven. At six foot two and 170 pounds, Sven hailed directly from Sweden and was nicknamed "The Nordic God." He wore his white-blond hair chin-length, perfectly framing his rectangular face. While we danced to "Beds Are Burning"—a song condemning the exploitation of Australia's aboriginal land and people—I stared longingly at Sven, the poster boy for colonialism, hoping he would consider exploiting me. (Yes, I know, Britain colonized Australia, but he was super white and tall, which is how I picture all colonists. Plus, history was not my best subject at the time.)

The next morning, I hit the hallways hoping to hear some positive gossip about me floating around school. Sadly, there were no reports of Sven having been mesmerized by a spiral-permed eleventh grader exposing her belly, scar and all, at a rock show. But there was an interesting development. Sven's friend Tommy had misread my coquettish gaze and assumed I was making eyes at him all night. Sure, maybe I needed better aim, but I was getting results, nonetheless. Tommy told Carrie, who sat behind me in chemistry, that he wanted to take me out to a movie.

Tommy was not a Nordic god. He was like Sven's evil twin. Also tall, but with chin-length curly brown hair, Tommy wore homemade T-shirts that read EAT THE RICH and TOO DRUNK TO FUCK. Even though he was always on the honor roll, I was perceived as the good girl that he was corrupting. I coveted that role; it made me feel like I was taking a risk—like if I dated him I wouldn't have to sign up for

Outward Bound. I told Carrie to tell Tommy that I was free Friday night after ballet class.

We went to see *Boyz in the Hood* at the local movie theater—which, from the standpoint of two white kids living in suburban Canada, could easily be classified as a foreign film—and then spent the rest of the night sitting in Tommy's truck talking about how cool we were. We immediately became a thing. We dressed in matching all-black attire and were idolized by all the weirdo cliques in high school. Tommy gave me a thumb ring, prompting Andrea (pronounced Un-DREY-uh), a brainiac who sat across from me in social studies, to dreamily ask if we would get married one day.

"Married?" I sneered. "Nooooo. Marriage is a failed, old-fashioned institution. Maybe we'll have a commitment ceremony and get matching tattoos, but I'm never getting *married*."

I pronounced the word with such contempt it might as well have been "bestiality" or "cruise ship vacation." Marriage was too mainstream for us, but I was positive that Tommy and I would be together forever. Or at least until graduation.

My mother despised Tommy and his never-ending three-chord guitar strumming in our family room almost as much as she hated her own boyfriend, Ivan. While Ivan spent his time drinking at the local Legion, Tommy was moshing at all-ages punk rock shows. That winter, my mom and I lived together like estranged roommates, avoiding each other as often as we could. She'd go to work, clean the house, and head over to Ivan's, despite how much she pretended to loathe him. I bounced from school, to ballet, to punk gigs with Tommy. However, by spring, our mother-daughter relationship temporarily improved when I was chosen to dance in the Alberta Ballet's production of *Swan Lake*. I'd worked my ass off (almost literally) in ballet for that opportunity, partially out of guilt from being constantly reminded how much those lessons cost. My mother was so proud of me that for an entire month I could do no wrong. But I found a way.

The morning of the final dress rehearsal and first performance, my mother opened the door of my basement bedroom to make sure I was awake, and found Tommy in bed with me, both of us naked, entwined in each other's arms.

At the sight of my mother, I sat up so fast I nearly fainted.

Until that moment, Tommy and I had been employing what we thought was a fool proof system for his escape if he spent the night: I'd set the alarm for 5:00 AM, then we'd quietly creep up the stairs together and I would silence the wind chime that hung strategically close to the back door (my mom was no dummy) while he slipped out. Tommy would then put his truck in neutral and let it roll past a couple of houses before starting the engine. For whatever reason, this time we slept through the alarm. Even mastermind criminals slip up once in a while. Perhaps I was exhausted from months of long dance rehearsals, and since Tommy didn't really give a shit about getting caught, it was possible that he carelessly shut it off and fell back to sleep.

Unlike Tommy, I wasn't used to getting in trouble. I'd never been grounded or had my privileges revoked, so I had no idea what to expect. Even though my mom was permissive by today's standards, she still had old-fashioned ideas about sex and certainly did not condone having it under her roof, especially by her youngest. And it was clear by the look on her face that she was sure that *we'd had sex*. If she only knew. My mom glared at Tommy, her eyes ablaze. "Get out of my house, NOW!" she commanded in a low, threatening tone normally reserved for my wayward older brother. "And take your guitar with you!" She slammed my door shut and stormed back upstairs.

Tommy wiped the sleep out of his eyes, turned to me, and said, "Babe, do I really need to go?"

"Yes! Go!!" I yelled in a panic and shoved him out of my room.

I could hear my mom angrily stomping around above me as I quickly got ready, gathering up my tulle skirt and white-swan-feather hairpiece. I ran up the stairs and whisked by her to wait in the car, terrified, with my head tucked into my jacket. My stomach lurched with nausea in anticipation of her wrath, but she didn't say one word during the entire drive—not that I'd have been able to hear her over the pounding of my heart. By the time I entered the studio to warm up, I was already sweating.

Before rehearsal, I confided in some of the ballerinas that I was about to get thrown out of my house. In reality, there was no way my mother was going to kick me and my pointe shoes to the curb, but it was the worst punishment I could imagine. As they rehairsprayed their buns, some of the swans exchanged looks of disdain. They didn't understand how I could waste my time with this guy—he wasn't even a choreographer, body image therapist, or amphetamine dealer. Others consoled me by saying that I could totally come live at their houses, secretly, in their basements; they wouldn't have to feed me much. I was a ballerina.

The lights dimmed at the Jubilee Theater and the orchestra swelled. I *pas de bourréed* onto the stage, took my place by the lake, and folded my wrists in front of my long white tutu as swans do. I could feel my mother's eyes watching me, wrestling with the fact that her little ballerina was growing up way too fast for her taste.

After the curtain call, I didn't want to leave the stage. I was safe up there in that fantasy world, where if things didn't work out, you could jump into a shimmery lake. But the house lights flickered, signaling it was time to face the real music.

Other than giving me a stiff hug and a tight smile of congratulations after the performance, my mom ignored me and engaged the other parents about the show. She was silent on our walk to the car. As we drove home, I patiently waited to receive my sentence. Finally my mother said, "So. What do you want to know about sex?"

I didn't want to know anything about sex from *her*, but I detected it might be my road to forgiveness. So I half-listened. What could she possibly tell me that I didn't already know from Banff or *Swank?*

My performance in *Swan Lake* was my coming-of-age ceremony, the bat mitzvah I would never have. My mom may have realized that I'd be leaving the nest soon, regardless of how much she yelled at me now, because in addition to telling me that "a gentle lover is a good lover" during that uncomfortable drive home, she also softened her stance on Tommy sleeping over, as long as I asked for her consent first. None of my other friends enjoyed anything even close to this level of freedom. No grounding? No television privileges revoked? No living in Nicole Peter's basement? Or is it simply impossible to be angry with your daughter when she's dressed up like a sad swan? Either way, investing in those expensive ballet lessons *was* money well spent.

CHAPTER 5

TOMMY, CAN YOU HEAR ME?

My Australian friend Tai couldn't believe that Tommy and I had never heard of the movie *Dogs in Space*. It was an odd little film about a bunch of suburban punk rockers living in a communal house, all searching for the true meaning of anarchy. Tai said it was so *us*. It certainly struck a chord with me, even though it was actually more of a cautionary tale about overdosing on heroin while pretending to be in a band. Nevertheless, I was deeply affected by the style and rebellious tone of the movie and wanted to be like those punk rockers—minus the shooting heroin part. I dreamed of squatting in a half-finished condo with other nonconformists, retaliating against capitalism, commercialism, and *the man*—whomever that was. I would learn to play the mandolin, make hemp jewelry, and have stimulating conversations while sitting on milk crates. I could even sew pillows for the crates out of vintage fabric. My fellow squat-mates and I would stage spontaneous political performances in public spaces and create art installations using tarnished kitchen utensils. I envisioned myself as a composite of Dian Fossey, Wendy of Prince's "Wendy and Lisa" fame, and a Banana Boat suntan lotion model: smart, edgy, and hot. At the time, I thought these aspirations made me different.

The fact that Tommy and I had met at a Midnight Oil concert and were obsessed with *Dogs in Space* clearly meant that we were destined to travel to Australia together. Tommy said it best: "Babe, we should go there so we can be us."

We weren't just a couple; we were style icons. We embraced the outcast archetype and thought of ourselves as the suburban version of Sid and Nancy. Again, minus the heroin. And the stabbing. The land down under seemed like the ultimate place to further cultivate our alternative personas.

Moments after my mom noticed that I'd triple-pierced my ears, I told her I was planning to take a year off after high school and travel around Australia with Tommy.

"Take those earrings out now, and you're not going anywhere," she said, with the intolerance of a retired drill sergeant and mother of six.

But it wasn't going to be that easy. After all, I was a strong-minded and determined seventeen-year-old. "Mom, I'm not taking the earrings out. You can't make me. *And,*" I added smugly, "I'm going. It's too late. I already bought my plane ticket."

She knew I meant it because we were cut from the same stubborn cloth. She quickly forgot the six new holes in my head and started bargaining like a recovering alcoholic at a New Year's Eve party, offering me an all-expenses-paid trip to Holland to see her side of the family if I gave up on Australia. She's lucky I didn't take her up on that; a free trip to Amsterdam for a girl like me would have landed me in the sequel to *Dogs in Space* way more quickly than backpacking through Melbourne. But I refused her bribes. I was going to Australia. I would fund my own trip. She couldn't stop me.

The problem was that Tommy and I weren't really getting along. Our relationship was increasingly volatile and dramatic. We fought constantly, although I can't imagine about what since we didn't share money, an apartment, or children. That said, it came to light that Tommy took his bad-boy image seriously; he was increasingly jealous and totally unpredictable. For instance, one afternoon while I was working at my mother's grocery store, he stormed in, wrestled me to the ground, pinned my hands to the floor, and asked if I was flirting with his friend Raj. The answer was yes, but again, it was probably not the best time for the truth.

"Get the fuck off of me!" I yelled as loud as I could and wiggled out of his grip. "Are you fucking crazy? Never touch me like that again. *Ever!*"

"I won't as long as you never talk to Raj again," he threatened.

"Don't be insane. You can't tell someone to do that. What the fuck is wrong with you?"

He slumped into a chair like a six-year-old boy forced to share his favorite toy. His outburst should have raised some major red flags, but hey—he'd never done anything like that before, and I figured I could handle him. I took my "survivor" image a little too seriously.

THE SCHOOL YEAR was wrapping up, and Tommy and I were invited to a country club for the Honors Society banquet, a grade-based night of awards and overcooked chicken breasts. After receiving our engraved plaques, Tommy and I started to needle each other. He thought I was ignoring him by talking to the other dorks, and I was annoyed that he kept nagging me about leaving early to catch some crappy hardcore band downtown. The result was a huge fight, where I ran out of the dining room in tears. Tommy followed and our argument continued in the car until I noticed he was driving the wrong direction, toward the outskirts of town.

"What are you doing?" I demanded.

All I got was a maniacal smile.

I tensed up. I didn't like this weird control game and demanded that he pull over immediately. Which he did, very calmly. I hadn't really planned on what to do next, but it seemed like the only thing to do was to get out, which I did. He leaned over, presumably to talk me into getting back in the car, but he pulled the passenger's door shut instead, did a U-turn, and accelerated back into town. I stood on the side of the highway in awe, clutching my golden plaque. Not exactly the poster child for the Honors Society.

I walked along the highway for about half an hour, wondering how long it would take me to get home, when Tommy returned. I got back in the car, defeated, and tried to pretend like the whole thing had never happened. But I couldn't. The next morning, I woke up with a clear head and a solid conclusion that traveling with Tommy to the other side of the planet was a terrible idea. I kept hearing this TV announcer's voice in my head say, "If you liked being abandoned on a highway outside of Calgary, you'll love being left at Ayers Rock!"

Tommy and I had plans to hang out at his house because his parents were out of town. His "house" was a mobile home on a farm ten miles outside of city limits, and a few miles past the last remaining drive-in movie theater. He picked me up and we grabbed some Taco Bell for dinner.

We were sitting at the dining room table, finishing our tacos, when he brought out some of our travel brochures to review. My stomach sunk. I couldn't do it. I wanted to avoid this moment but knew it was inevitable. I took a deep breath. "Tommy, I . . . this isn't working. I can't do it anymore." I paused, then closed with the headline. "I want to break up."

As I sat there holding my breath, knowing he would *not* react well to this, I could see the rage building inside of him. Within seconds, he exploded into angry tears. He started circling the room and raving like a madman.

"No! No! No! We're going to *stay* together, whether you like it or not!"

That didn't sound . . . reasonable.

"What's so wrong with me?!" he shouted. "Tell me exactly what is so wrong?" And then he tossed me a sheet of paper. "Write them down! All of them. Write them down!"

He looked different to me. All of a sudden I had no idea what he was capable of. My brain started to go to fearful places. *Don't most murders happen on farms?* It just didn't feel real; it was like I was in a movie—the prequel to *Trailer Park of Terror.* Tommy left the room to blow his nose, and my instincts told me to flee, pronto. Unfortunately, I didn't have a car or a plan, so I simply ran. I tore out of the trailer, leaving the screen door flapping behind me, and darted down the half-mile dirt road that led to the highway.

Panting on the dark highway again, I remembered that there was a lonely pay phone near the drive-in movie theater about fifteen minutes away, so I jogged toward it in my jelly shoes. Fishing around in the bottom of my purse, I found a bunch of pennies and one quarter. I thanked the spare-change gods and cursed Midnight Oil, *Dogs in Space,* and Sweden. The decision of who to call was simple: my friend Seth. Seth was the kind of guy who was always up for anything.

"Hey, Seth, it's Ophira!" I said, as if he had won a prize.

"Oh, hi!" He sounded genuinely happy to hear my voice.

"Something weird happened between Tommy and me and . . . could you come pick me up?" I tried to sound nonchalant.

"Sure. Are you at home or something?"

"I'm in the parking lot of the Mac's Convenience Store off of Highway 45 right before the drive-in movie theater." I shoved all the information together to make it sound like a composed request rather than a cry for help.

"*Um.* Okay. Where is that again?"

I gave him expert directions, since I'd driven that route four hundred thousand times and knew exactly how long it would take. I hung up the phone, wiped the highway dirt from my face, and headed toward Mac's. It was about a twenty-minute walk. If I made it with a few minutes to spare, I could buy a Slurpee.

It was quiet on the street, almost deserted except for one other person up ahead walking a dog. They were a blur in the dark, so I slowed down to avoid encountering them. As I came a little closer, the dog walker turned around and transformed into a familiar figure: Tommy.

"O-phir-rahhhhh!" He howled my name like a Shakespearean villain and ran toward me. I'd never felt such a menacing moment, even later in life, when I was ping-ponging around strange men's apartments in New York City. Call me lucky. I spun around and ran in the other direction, into the trailer park. Tommy, chasing me, yelled, "I just want to know what is so wrong!" I wanted to shout back, "Well for one, you're chasing me!" but figured I should save my breath.

Adrenaline coursed through my body and gave me superhuman powers. I ran faster than I had at any track meet, terrified to be caught. I flashed forward to sprinting away from him in the outback as a kangaroo hopped by.

There is no way I'm going on a trip across the world with a crazy person! I thought, as I vaulted over a broken fence. I wasn't stupid.

I could hear Tommy's footsteps pounding behind me, his body triggering motion lights outside of the trailers. I jetéd over a small ravine and wondered, *Why couldn't I have dated Sven?* He might have chloroformed me, but at least he wouldn't have hunted me.

As I careened around the corner near the dumpsters behind Mac's, I saw a familiar-looking car pull into the parking lot, with a hippie redhead behind the wheel. It was Seth. He had perfect timing—*movie* timing. He spotted me and got out of the car.

"Hey, Ophira!" He waved at me with a relaxed smile.

"Get in the car! Start the car!" I screamed, barreling toward him. Seth's face turned from pale to panic as he slid back in and started the car. I rammed into the passenger's door but managed to swing it open, and threw myself into the green-gold mock-leather seats of Seth's hand-me-down Oldsmobile. He needed no additional command to "gun it" when he saw Tommy racing toward us.

"What the hell is going on?" he demanded.

"*Uh*, Tommy and I broke up," I muttered.

Wasn't that obvious?

As Tommy became a tiny figure in the rearview mirror, sweat and relief washed over me. I pleaded with Seth to let me stay at his place. I was too afraid to go home. At least I could take some solace in the fact that if Tommy dared wake up my mother, she'd kill him.

"Of course, no problem," he said, sounding a little stoned.

A half hour later, I was safe in the warmth of Seth's room and his arms. As it turned out, he had a thing for me. I must have had a hunch when I called him at midnight to rescue me. He was my hero. I slipped into his bed wearing a pair of his boxers and a T-shirt, figuring the best way to thank Seth, in lieu of gas money, was to have sex with him. I had a knack for moving on . . . rather quickly. Why not delay dealing with the aftermath of the evening by engaging in a little pleasant distraction? Maybe this was no coincidence; maybe the forces of nature brought me to Seth on purpose. But when I went to kiss him, he pushed me away, claiming my timing was "all wrong."

"Why?" I asked. "We're here now," I said, alluding to this magical coincidence I conjured up in my head, one we'd be fools not to take advantage of.

Seth sat up in his futon. "Ophira, I'm going to Europe for a year. Tomorrow."

Dumbfounded, I suddenly noticed a huge packed knapsack, with a hand-sewn Canadian flag on the front, propped against the wall. I nodded and hugged Seth. And we slept.

I woke up to sun streaming through the A-frame windows and Seth scurrying around his room in final preparations for his big trip. He drove me home, and when I wished him well, it felt like we were parting colleagues who had worked together on a project that never got funding. My mother saw me from the window and ran out the front door waving and yelling at me.

"What the hell happened to you?" she demanded. "That good-for-nothing boyfriend of yours knocked on the door at three in the morning looking for you, and then sat out in front of the house half of the night waiting for you!"

I was disappointed she didn't kill him.

"We broke up, Mom."

It was all I needed to say. She shook her head, fed up by my ongoing teenage drama, but I detected a small smile on her face. She was pleased to finally be rid of that good-for-nothing Tommy.

I plopped onto the couch and buried my head in a pillow. What was I going to do? I was certain that my life was going to be better now that he was out of the picture, but the trip was ruined. He was probably canceling it as I lay there. Wait. Why couldn't I still go? People travel by themselves all the time. I had saved up all my own money, and at seventeen I was a smart, independent woman who could run really, really fast. I was ready to shed my small-town skin, upgrade from trailer trash in the boyfriend department, and discover who I was in relation to the rest of the world. And I'd do it alone.

FIJIAN WATERS RUN DEEP

That summer, I took a job at a do-it-yourself jewelry shop called Beadworks to raise money for my big walkabout through Australia. I maneuvered around that store in ill-fitting vintage dresses and hand-woven tribal fabrics, spouting my philosophy du jour—primarily, that I didn't believe in God or love because they were constructs built to keep women down. That was until Michael, the guitar guy, walked into the bead store and ruined everything.

I knew *of* Michael before I actually met him. He offered jazz guitar lessons at my high school, and every time he showed up in the band room, my friends Cheryl and Diane, who played saxophone, would swoon. They'd gush about his boyish good looks and recount his witty asides and observations, but my curiosity was not in the least bit piqued. Going gaga over any guitar player—especially an "older" one (he was the ripe old age of twenty at the time)—seemed so cliché.

For my graduation photo, I had braided tiny skull beads into my hair. Clearly I was marching to the beat of my own cow bell. If I were going to crush out on an older guy, it would be a forensic archaeologist, or at the very least an oboe player. So when Michael came into the jewelry shop a year later, I played it cool in my purple Guatemalan pants.

He complimented the beads in my hair. I told him they were baby-hamster skulls. He laughed and said I was funny. In that moment, I noticed his big sapphire-blue eyes framed by four-inch lashes. I felt like a fawn caught in the headlights of his speeding car. If I didn't look away, I'd be creamed.

Too late.

As we talked, I started to fall under his spell. Michael was different. He wore a blazer. He didn't seem full of angst, tormented by the problems in Tibet, or on an eternal search for the best 'shrooms. He wasn't rebelling against anything—just trying to make a living playing jazz. By comparison, all my past boyfriends seemed like hacky-sack-obsessed adolescents who were excited to find a bong that matched their bed sheets. The more I talked to Michael, the more his sweet demeanor seemed to wash away my layers of black eyeliner and tough, too-cool-for-school exterior to reveal a more innocent Ophira who still wanted to be a ballerina. I couldn't believe it. Was I really falling for his smooth jazz shit?

Despite all the edginess I thought I possessed, I caught myself giggling at his cheesy jokes while I attempted to make him a bracelet out of leather and some masculine-looking beads, which I've since learned is an oxymoron. He let me put my creation on his wrist, and I joked that we were now married in Burkina Faso or something. He laughed again.

"So how much does a Burkina Faso marriage bracelet cost?" he asked.

"Oh no, it's on me," I said.

"Are you cereal?"

"Totally!"

"Really? What kind?"

And then he elbowed me, cracking up that I fell so willingly into that classic little word gag. I laughed along with him, although it was the first time I'd ever heard it.

"Okay, at least let me buy you a drink. Oh! Do you want to come see me play tomorrow night? I'm in this superfunkyfragilistic show band, Penguins on Broadway. We've got a gig at Rosie's tomorrow night. What says you?" There was something about the way he talked and joked that reminded me a little of Bill Murray.

"I'd love to," I said hesitantly, "but, *uh*, I'm underage." I was so embarrassed by my youth.

He winked and twirled his bracelet. "Don't worry. I gotcha."

The jazz club was the most adult place I'd been to, with the exception of the Philharmonic and Chippendales. The clientele looked grown-up, the kind of people who recently took down their British flag in favor of curtains for their windows. It was a welcome switch from all-ages punk gigs and the plaid-clad pseudo-skinheads I'd been subjected to for the past year. I sat at my cloth-covered table and clumsily ordered a glass of red wine of some sort from the intimidating wine list. There wasn't one other person even close to my own age in the club. I loved it.

The music was a different story. Forget about trying to like jazz; I couldn't even understand the musical arrangement. It sounded disjointed and messy, like someone took a heaping box of notes and threw them all over the floor. I didn't recognize any of the tunes, but I pretended to be engaged. That changed the moment Michael launched into his guitar solo. He played, looking at me with such intensity, it seemed that every note professed his love.

I relinquished control. My body felt like a chemistry set with all its Bunsen burners set on high. Had Cheryl and Diane been there in that moment, they would have taken one look at me, nodded their heads knowingly, and whispered, "Told you so."

The show ended and Michael shook hands with the regulars, then walked over to my table with a couple of glasses of wine. Both starstruck and lovestruck, I tripped over my words trying to express how much I loved his playing and the show and the bar and that he was just . . . amazing! He suggested I drink up so he could drive me home.

Yes, sir!

We sat parked in front of my house, talking and laughing at his jokes, until we hit that pause in the conversation that I'd been waiting for. Michael looked at me, his blue eyes filled with intent, gathered me in his arms out of my bucket seat, and, with the gearshift between us, kissed me hard—not with spastic excitement, but with jazzy passion. It was perfect. I never wanted to get out of the car. But I did . . . three hours later.

The next night we saw a movie, but all I remember is the electricity I felt while holding his hand in the dark theater. Afterward we went to his place, or rather his parents' basement, where Michael not only lived but also had constructed an entire music studio. He put on a variety of Miles Davis and Coltrane CDs, occasionally picking up his guitar to play a riff here and there. I'm pretty sure I just sat there with a big smile plastered on my face and big hearts in my eyes. Soon we were having sex, right on the carpeted floor of his soundproofed studio, and finally my sister's prophecy came true. I felt something this time, and it was downright incredible. Although I didn't have a huge sample size to compare it to, our sexual chemistry bubbled out of the test tube. This was it. The real thing. True love. A perfect match. I'd done it. I'd found it.

Life was magical. I actually saw sparkles in almost everything I looked at. He taught me about jazz, we explored museums, and we had tons of sex. Since we clicked so well in the bedroom, we consequently spent a great deal of time there, putting certain Prince songs on repeat. To this day, the first few chords of "When 2 R in Love" from *The Black Album* share a sexual trigger with tinted Halloween hairspray.

I don't think Michael had ever met someone who idolized him the way I did. I told him repeatedly that I couldn't believe someone like *him* could like someone like *me*, reinforcing that he could do better. Luckily he adored my worship, and after a couple of weeks together, he confessed that he was falling in love with me.

Like any seventeen-year-old girl head over heels in love, I wanted nothing more than to cancel my trip to Australia and stay with

Michael . . . for eternity. And like any typical twenty-two-year-old guy, Michael insisted that if I didn't go, I would be making a huge mistake. "But what about us? What if I go and I lose you?" I implored. How could he stand a year of celibacy? How could *I*? He reassured me that nothing could shake what we had. It would be romantic— pining for each other. He also reminded me how much time I'd spent planning and saving, and he warned me like the wizened elder he was that I might never get this opportunity again. He assured me that we'd write and talk regularly, and the distance would make our relationship grow even stronger. It was going to be the trip of a lifetime, one that I'd never forget.

He was right about that.

Like a devoted cult member, I clung to his every word and obediently started packing.

I wrote him every day on that trip. According to his count, I sent him seventy-six letters, all ten pages or more.

He sent me four.

The trip itself got off to a rough start. After choking back tears at the airport, afraid to reveal that after all this effort I was scared and wanted to go back home, I waved good-bye to Michael and my family and dragged my backpack through security. Eventually, I made my way down the skinny aisle of the plane, dabbing my eyes, slumped into my aisle seat, and let out a huge sigh. I turned to acknowledge my seat neighbor and screamed. It was Tommy.

Apparently, he'd decided to go on the trip alone too. *Why hadn't that occurred to me?!* I looked at him, completely dazed. I thought for sure he would cancel. He was only going on the trip because I initiated it, and I never imagined he'd be able to afford the fare on his own. Evidently I was wrong.

He was also at a total loss. It hadn't dawned on either of us that this could happen. We'd clearly underestimated how like-minded we were. Since neither of us had bothered to create a new itinerary, we were stuck together not only on this first leg to Hawaii but also on all subsequent flights to Fiji, the Cook Islands, and New Zealand, before hitting Australia.

You can't run away on an airplane, but you can beg for a new seat, which I did immediately. After our epic breakup, we completely avoided each other, to the point where I wondered if he'd left town. I just didn't expect the answer would be yes, via my plane to Australia.

He seemed perfectly happy to watch me huff and hastily gather my stuff to move rows. The flight attendant directed me to a new seat at the rear of the plane. It was the last aisle, so it was a nonreclining seat, opposite the bathroom. As if that weren't bad enough, the seat next to me was occupied by a nervous woman holding a fussy newborn. Perfect. At least the kid cried most of the trip so I didn't have to.

Tommy must have shot off that airplane the moment we landed, because I didn't see him in the baggage area. I'd made friends with a couple of backpackers who were also sitting in the back and followed them to a cheap hostel near Waikiki. I didn't mention anything about Tommy to them. It was my way of writing him out of my future, at least for the next twenty-four hours. I bided my time by walking along the beach, perusing tourist shops, and writing to Michael—basically waiting to get back to the airport so I could change my seat assignment for the next leg out.

When I didn't spot Tommy in the departure lounge, I figured he'd missed the flight. Good. I changed my seat and joined the line for the bathrooms, relieved he wasn't there. He was a stain on my relationship past, and I never wanted to see him again. This was my vacation, my trip of a lifetime. But then, whether by coincidence or design, there he was, standing right behind me in line.

My body pulsed with rage feeling his presence so close.

I turned around to face him and practically spat, "So. How was Hawaii?"

"Babe, it was so cool!" he said, raising his eyebrows to add emphasis.

How dare he call me babe! And how dare he look so . . . so . . . *smug.* He bragged about how surprisingly good he was at surfing, and how he caught a fish while deep sea diving, and what fun he'd had drinking on the beach late into the night—mai tais with models! *Seriously?* I thought. *All that in twenty-four hours?* Part of me wanted to call bullshit on his stories, or at least ask for names, but instead I tuned him out as he further embellished his exploits, and began plotting my next move. Now I understood what we were doing. It was a competition: Whoever was having a better trip was having a better postbreakup life. The game was on, and I was in last place. That was about to change.

My makeover plan was twofold. First, I required a physical transformation in the form of a golden tan. Once we landed in Fiji, I hit the beach slathered in SPF 2 and jumped into the ocean. While floating in the warm azure shallows, I conceived the second part of my plan: go on an exotic adventure, like hunting for white men with Maoris, or do something dangerous that no mere tourist would do.

As I was dreaming up activities—like bushwhacking my way through the jungle to photograph myself draped in rare poisonous snakes or harvesting the summer's first crop of cassava with an Aboriginal tribal leader, I felt a sharp stinging on my torso, like little razors raking across my stomach. I looked down to see red welts quickly forming on my midriff and ran to the lifeguard-on-duty in a panic. He gave me a condescending laugh and said I'd been stung by baby jellyfish. *Baby jellyfish?!* Being bit by baby jellyfish was about as pathetic as being devoured by a teddy bear. I didn't plan for jellyfish, nor did I plan for the fragility of my lily-white Canadian skin, which had never been exposed to the intense equatorial sun and tropical humidity.

By evening, the jelly-baby stings were out-pained by a flaming-hot sunburn. It was so bad that my only relief was soaking in a bath filled with baking soda—at the hostel. Considering that hostel "bathtubs" are primarily used for feet and pets, I was lucky I didn't walk away with fleas and a staph infection.

By the end of the week, I had two additional problems: little blisters had formed on my back, which the Fijian pharmacist identified as a heat rash, and my big toe was infected from the dampness and dirt that had collected in my closed-toe sandals. Closed-toe sandals made perfect sense in Calgary, but not so much in a place where you'd actually *need* sandals. I was given medicated white powder to sprinkle on my back, and iodine to treat my infection, which was a perfectly legitimate disinfectant, but it stained my toes a rust color. I struck quite the image: cherry red from head to toe, with a dusting of white on my shoulders, like sugar. I felt like a Willy Wonka reject.

Obviously, I needed new shoes, so I stopped by one of the sidewalk vendors and picked out a pair that looked like a trellis of black leather straps woven together. I put them on. *Hm.* Pretty stylish, pretty comfortable. They'd do. When I returned to the hostel, the girl at the front desk looked me up and down and asked, "Why are you wearing men's shoes?"

All of a sudden, it made sense why the vendor had a hard time finding my size. I looked down at them in a new light. Oh man, they *did* look like men's sandals. The kind an old Greek man would wear to fetch his morning paper. I was embarrassed by how much of a dumb tourist I was. My face would have turned red if it wasn't already.

Then there was my expensive spiral-permed hair. It was an increasing burden, knotting and wrapping itself into dreadlocks because of the dense humidity. A haircut would make me feel better. I thought of Zoe, a modern ballet dancer that Michael had told me he found really attractive. She sported a short, elegant, bi-level bob. *That's it!* I thought. I would be free of my wasp nest, *and* Michael would find me irresistible. Done.

Word to the wise: Never get your hair cut out of desperation, especially in a foreign country.

I went into town, which consisted of one dusty street, and walked into the first beauty parlor I saw. Three lovely women welcomed me, but we suffered a language barrier, and they tilted their heads in confusion at the word *bob*. They handed me a stack of outdated hairstyling magazines and told me to point. I found a couple of photos that were close to what I was after, especially if you employed a bit of imagination. They smiled and nodded enthusiastically in response, so it seemed we were good to cut.

I got my hair cut all right. They chopped it right off, leaving just a few inches, each strand cut a little differently. I didn't recognize my own reflection. I looked like a young boy who'd been mistaken for a garden hedge. At least it went with my mandals.

Next stop: a Fijian wig store.

As I shuffled back toward the hostel, where I could lose it in the privacy of my bunk bed, I contemplated whether I should just surrender and hightail it back to Calgary and Michael's arms. I was no Zoe, but I was confident he'd lovingly stick by my side as my hair grew out and my sunburn faded.

Then I heard an all-too-familiar voice. "Hey! Hey! Ophira! Ophira!"

Great. Nothing like adding insult to hair injury.

Tommy appeared in front of me like a shitty magic trick. I let out another big sigh as he slowly took me in: All in all, I looked like I'd barely survived first day on deck as an entry-level pirate.

He, on the other hand, was sun kissed rather than scorched and looked better than ever.

"Oh my god, Ophira," he said. "I barely recognize you. You've totally changed!"

I know he didn't mean it as a compliment, but I chose to hear it that way. For better or worse, I couldn't deny that things were changing. If I returned to Calgary now, my life would go back to what it was. The fatalist in me mused that all the crap Tommy and I had gone through was preparing us for this moment, so he could say that to me. *You've totally changed.* Yes, I had. It wasn't how I thought I would, but everything was certainly different.

I brightened up and asked him how he was doing. He was fine, hanging out with more models, drinking more mai tais, being surprisingly good at more things. Whatever—it didn't matter anymore. Our lives were on different trajectories. We had crossed that point where we could move on without petty resentments, or even longing. Our hug good-bye was friendly and light, and I somehow knew I wouldn't see him again during the trip. I think he did too. We both had new lives to get back to, and I felt reinvigorated to continue with my life-altering trip that would surely make Michael proud of me.

CHAPTER 7

THE WHORE OF FRASER ISLAND

If there were a travel brochure for my year abroad, it would read "Australia: A Series of Distractions in between Calling Michael." I really was living the trip through his eyes, seeking out experiences for the sole purpose of relaying them back to him later. I had cinched myself so tightly in a corset designed to win his approval, sooner or later a ribbon was bound to snap.

The trip itself wasn't as exotic as I'd imagined. Being a seventeen-year-old tourist in Australia was more Miami Beach than Madagascar. As the months passed, it became clear that I wouldn't be dancing with the Aborigines or walking the Songlines. My road to cultural enlightenment and spiritual fulfillment was paved with poorly rolled spliffs and limbo contests.

Two months before I was due to return home, I saw a flyer on the hostel's bulletin board advertising a trip to Fraser Island. "Camp in the rainforest! Drive in Land Rovers on the beach! Enjoy an off-the-beaten-path adventure in paradise!" This was the piece of the puzzle I'd been searching for, so I signed up.

The next day, I found myself in a Land Rover wedged between a Kiwi, a Brit, and eight other backpackers, driving on the as-advertised white sandy beaches. But my heart sank when the guitar came out for the mandatory sing-along of "American Pie" around the campfire. There was no escaping spring break. The guys—most of them bona fide men, ranging from twenty-five to thirty-five—were making overt advances on all the girls, including me, even with my altar boy–chic hair.

As the Southern Cross illuminated the sky, cases of beer and pints of gin magically appeared, signaling the opening ceremony of the drinking Olympics. We were all expected to go for the gold.

I wasn't going to leave the group, wander into the forest, and write in my journal like an antisocial shut-in, so I figured, if you can't beat 'em, drink their booze. Five plastic water bottles of gin and Orange Crush later, I guzzled a Lite beer and smoked a joint in preparation for the drinking game, an athletic event where we put our hands on a beach ball, spun around three times, and ran as fast as we could toward the headlights of the Land Rover. The car radio was blaring pop music, and everyone was hooting and staggering in the sand. It was like a frat party without being in college, and I was having a blast.

The next thing I knew, the sun was peeking out from the horizon, and people began to crash on the beach. Still fully awake, walking the fine line between drunk and distilled, I decided to go for a stumble near the ocean. Trying to keep my balance while sinking in the sand, I heard a male voice call, "Hi!" It was one of the Brits from the group. We stood quietly near the lapping waves, the first rays of sun warming our feet, and he leaned in to kiss me. I pulled away ever so slightly, but quickly submitted to how good it felt, sloppily kissing back. For months, I'd been skirting real abandon on this trip, so I welcomed the opportunity to give in and let go. What's a little make-out session between strangers, right? Isn't that on the subitinerary of every back-packer's trip abroad? But the next thing I knew, we were lying down on the sand, naked. Then we were having sex on the beach. It felt like grinding pepper.

I woke inside the oven of burning nylon that was his tent. My head throbbed, my throat was parched from my lips to my stomach, and the scent of fermented liquor oozed from my pores. Peeling my eyes open, I shuddered as the memories slowly crept in.

Had I really cheated on Michael? With *this* guy? Some snoring, Beatle-loving, slightly pudgy, ginger-haired Brit? It wasn't a night-mare. Fuck. *Fuck!* Shame washed over my soul. I'd ruined everything. Ruined my perfect relationship. Become the stereotype of a stupid seventeen-year-old girl who drank too much and screwed some guy. I didn't even know his name! This wasn't a rehearsal. I wasn't in boy-friend previews anymore. Michael was the real thing, and I'd destroyed it in one dumb night.

But in reality, I had no idea what it really meant to ruin some-thing. Not yet.

Plucking the Brit's sweaty arm off my naked body, I shimmied into my shorts and went for another walk to figure things out. Along the forest path, I spotted an iconic red pay phone nestled between a palm tree and a giant fern. *It must be a sign.* I collect-called Michael.

I didn't know what I was going to say, but before I could sputter a desperate hello, he said, "I have a big surprise for you!"

That made two of us.

"I'm going to come meet you in Los Angeles on your way back. I'll drive down, pick you up at the airport, and then we can make our way back home together up the coast."

He also mentioned that this was an extra big deal because it would be his first trip with a girlfriend. *Ever.*

I was stunned that the universe would actually reward me after what I'd done.

I replied, "I can't wait!"

AS THEY SAY, there are no atheists in foxholes, and for the next two months I made promises to God, the universe, dead relatives, and the laws of science that I wouldn't screw up again. If I could get through this, I pledged to become the archetype of the ideal, faithful, doting girlfriend.

At a hostel in Auckland, two days before my flight to LA, I woke up startled by a creeping thought. I did some mental menstrual math, only to confirm my worst fear: Holy shit. I might be pregnant.

Okay, Ophira, don't freak out. I steeled myself against panic and went into troubleshooting mode. I could figure this out. I was plucky and self-reliant, right? And I was still off the grid for the next forty-eight hours. God and my dead relatives wouldn't let me down. They *couldn't*. Michael and I were meant to be.

With the kind of conviction a better person would reserve for something really important, like peace in the Middle East, I ran down to the front desk of the hostel and asked to borrow their equivalent of the Yellow Pages. I flipped to the "Family Planning" section and let my fingers do the walking. In bold, a clinic advertised free pregnancy tests for all New Zealand citizens. *Free to citizens . . . Hmmm.* Inspiration struck, and I hatched a plan.

I'd learn the accent.

I'd master the northern–New Zealand accent, pose as a local, and get a free exam. Simple! I didn't bother to consider yet what I would do if the results of the exam were positive. I just focused on the first step, which consisted of spending the day milking as much conversation as I could from cashiers and traffic cops, then imitating their lilt.

Word to the wise: The New Zealander accent is subtle.

The next morning, I put on my cleanest clothes and marched into the clinic.

"G'day," I said. "Oi was theenking oi might need a teest to see if oi'm pregguhs."

The nurse smiled and invited me into her office. She closed the door behind us, whipped around, and in a perfect New Zealand accent that sounded nothing like mine, said, "I know you're not from around here, so why don't you tell me what's going on?"

The sheepskin rug had been pulled out from under me. I broke down and told her everything—about Michael, the bead store, and Penguins on Broadway, building to the moment at Fraser Island and the nameless Brit who got me here; but most important, I told her I couldn't lose the love of my life. "I never thought I'd let this happen!" I wailed. The nurse handed me a tissue, patted me on the back, and gave me the free test.

Fifteen minutes later, which is four years in pregnancy-scare time, she announced, "Congratulations. You're not pregnant. Just a bit overstressed."

"But promise me that when you get home, you'll tell your boyfriend everything." She gave me a meaningful, motherly look.

What?! Oh no. I wasn't doing *that*. The problem was over. My pleas to the universe had been answered—or I'd somehow willed myself to not be pregnant. Whatever the case, it was over. No one would ever know. But I nodded yes and she said, "Good luck," and probably shook her head as she tossed my paperwork in the garbage.

The next day, I boarded a plane to Los Angeles. I was ecstatic. Wanting to look nice for Michael, I bought a cheap summer dress and a new pair of underwear at the airport. I'd read in a fashion magazine that if you wanted to be "fresh" for your companion, you should change your underwear right before landing.

My first whiff of LA smelled like cheap floral perfume, as opposed to the fragrant smell of the tropics I'd become accustomed to. My backpack, on the other hand, stank of body odor and was overflowing with dirty T-shirts, snow globes, and a six-foot didgeridoo

I'd brought back for Michael. After customs and immigration, I wheeled my baggage cart to the sliding doors leading to the main terminal. I was seconds away from seeing the man I'd spent an entire year pining over.

The doors *swooshed* open to a long ramp flanked with hundreds of people, all eagerly awaiting their friends and loved ones. As I walked up the slope in a parade of other arrivals, I worried that I wouldn't be able to spot him. It'd been a year—what if I couldn't recognize him? What if he was late? What if he'd decided not to come?

And then . . . there he was. The crowd around him fell away, and all I could see was Michael, waving and smiling at me. The Bunsen burners sparked to life, and I abandoned my baggage cart, which rolled back down the ramp, and ran shrieking like a lovestruck lunatic toward him.

The crowd around us went wild, clapping and cheering, as I flew into his arms, shaking and crying. I kept repeating, "Oh my god! Oh my god!" And Michael kept repeating, "It's gonna be okay. It's gonna be okay."

He kept anticipating that our elongated hug was over and would let go, but when I wouldn't, he'd rewrap his arms around me. Slowly I calmed myself down and gathered my abandoned bags and didgeridoo. We immediately went out for my favorite meal: grilled cheese sandwiches at Denny's.

It was difficult to know where to pick back up as a couple after so much time apart, so three hours later we were still laughing and replaying the scene I caused at the airport. The mixture of jet lag and the culture shock was jarring, and I didn't know where I was, who I was, or what anything meant. It was like I washed down a few Oxyco-done with a Jolt Cola. It was one in the morning in Anaheim, which meant noon the day before last month to me, and Michael suggested we scale the fence and hang out in our motel's now-closed pool. While treading water, he asked, "So, start from the beginning, and tell me about your trip."

I'd been living with him in my head for a year, but now that he was in front of me, we were strangers. We'd been apart from each other longer than we'd been together—by ten times. I suggested we get out of the pool and go back to our room. We had a lifetime of talking ahead of us.

We had sex on the stiff king-size motel bed, and I felt a stron-ger connection to him and my life, but we didn't exactly click like I remembered and romanticized. As I fell asleep, I tried to talk myself out of the profound loneliness that consumed my body. Surely, it must be just a side-effect of the time change.

The next morning we started our drive up the West Coast. For a week, we behaved like any new couple would on a road trip: holding hands, arguing over directions, and making up for lost time by having lots of sex. Somewhere outside of San Francisco, Michael turned to me and said, "It really hurts when I pee."

I didn't know exactly what that meant, and this was before Google, but I figured it might be STD-related. I started praying again, pleading with the higher powers to tell me why the hell they were doing this to me.

As the days passed, Michael complained that the pain was

getting worse. As for me, I didn't have any symptoms, unless you count *still not getting my period!*

My prayers turned to whisper-yelling.

Just past Santa Rosa, we stopped at a Walgreen's to see if they had a knowledgeable pharmacist who could prescribe a cream, a Magic 8 Ball—anything.

Back in the parking lot, we sat silently in the beige bucket seats of Michael's beat-up Volkswagen Jetta. He had some ointment in a bag, and I had a pack of gum and a pregnancy test stashed in my purse.

At last, he popped the question.

"I need to know. Were you with anyone else while in Australia?"

I wanted to pass out. The truth would not set me free. The truth would mean I'd lose him forever, and I couldn't let that happen. Why does he have to know about a useless one-night stand that even I don't remember? It had zero bearing on *our* future.

"No," I responded confidently.

"Good, good. Then it's just some naturally occurring bacteria or something, and we'll get it worked out."

But I wasn't really good with "good." What if he were seriously ill? What if he died or went blind because I withheld the truth?

I knew I couldn't say *no* and move on. I loved him. I didn't want to hurt him. But there was no way I was telling him that I cheated. Anything but that. How could I protect him AND our relationship? How could I tell him that I didn't mean it, that my decision maker was beyond drunk that night? That I was a dumb seventeen-year-old for a night? There had to be some way out of this.

You may not agree with what I did next, and I don't blame you, but it was the only thing I could come up with.

"Wait," I started, too feverish to continue.

"What?" he asked impatiently.

"I was raped."

As I said it, I looked down, not for effect, but because I couldn't look in his eyes.

I'm not proud of what I said, but I remember my twisted rationale: It absolved me of all responsibility. Plus, I figured he'd feel sorry for me.

Softly, Michael said, "What?" and then again a little louder, "*What* did you say?" His voice crescendoed as he pelted me with more and more questions.

"What the hell are you talking about?! Did you go to the police? Where was this? Why didn't you tell me?"

He grabbed me by the shoulders and demanded I tell him every detail of what happened.

Hesitantly, looking at him sideways, I told him about the excursion to Fraser Island and the nameless Brit, exaggerating certain aspects to make the story work with my fabrication. Michael stopped me mid-alibi and looked at me dead in the face with unsympathetic sapphire eyes.

"You're lying."

"How dare you say that to someone who's been raped!" I said, feigning indignation.

He didn't blink.

"You're lying."

It was my move.

I was officially out of moves.

"But it was awful. I got really, really drunk and—"

"'You got really, really drunk?'" he repeated slowly, while rubbing his face. I wanted to throw myself from the car—if only it were moving.

"Jesus Christ, Ophira," he said in a scary-soft voice. "You know, Ophira, I love you, but I am so disappointed in you."

He started the car and looked at me again, maybe for the last time.

"We can't be together now. It's over."

The cold words resonated in my head like a death knell. This was it. There was no REVERSE or BACK button. To make matters worse, I had to sit next to him in that car for at least three more days with my heart in my throat, living out my own *Swan Lake*. In my case, a Canadian goose lost in a storm of regret.

I spent the rest of the trip punishing myself, inwardly flogging every aspect of my personality, while Michael continued to complain about his undiagnosed infection. We went through our daily routines but hardly talked, making record time on the highway. There was no need to stop to take photos. A vacation with an STD in the backseat is a fast one.

Occasionally, the tension would break. At a self-serve gas station, I passed Michael some money and accidentally rolled the window up on his finger. He cried out in pain, and in an effort to fix it, I mistakenly rolled it up more. When I finally pulled the switch and released his hand, he laughed.

"What's next? Are you going to run me over?" he quipped.

"That would be too easy, right?" I nervously joked back, trying to share in the moment, but the smile quickly faded from his face, and we resumed the drive.

Somewhere close to Oregon, Michael had a sore throat and complained that the infection was taking over his body. I couldn't tell if he was honestly worried or was enjoying torturing me, but I'd reached my limit.

I insisted that we drive to a hospital to get a diagnosis. He resisted, claiming that they wouldn't be able to tell him anything definitive in such a short time. With my remaining young-adult resolve, I insisted that he follow the signs to the next hospital.

It was in a town called Eureka.

While he saw a doctor, I slumped in a waiting-room chair and aged a few years. Ten minutes later, he materialized with a bottle of tetracycline and very few answers. They told him he was suffering from an infection but didn't specify what kind. They suspected gonorrhea and asked him to tell his girlfriend to get herself checked out as soon as possible.

I was the infected body. The dirty girl. The Whore of Fraser Island.

I could not believe I screwed everything up with one stupid evening. I despised myself.

By the time we reached my house on a beautiful, sunny day in Calgary, Alberta, Canada, our relationship was dead and buried. My mother and her new boyfriend, Zeke, greeted us full of smiles and hugs. I didn't have the energy to return a fake smile as I lugged my beat-up backpack and beat-up heart through their happy-homecoming gauntlet and down to my old room. From my small basement window, I watched the tires on Michael's car spin and drive away with my now unrequited love and the didgeridoo.

For the next few weeks I talked to Michael on and off, agreeing with him that I was a terrible, terrible person—and begging him to take me back. As prescribed, I made a trip to the local health clinic, which was decorated with posters reading, SO YOU'RE CASUAL ABOUT SEX? ARE YOU CASUAL ABOUT DEATH? I swear that even the nurses gave me dirty looks.

They called with results a week later, and I braced myself for English syphilis, but was told that I had . . . nothing. I was completely healthy. In my warped mind, all I could think was that with this news, Michael would have to take me back.

I drove to his house. At first he didn't know quite what to say, but settled on, "It's probably lying dormant in your body, which happens, you know. The STD could flourish at any time."

My mind flashed forward sixty years. I was in a nursing home in a pink housecoat, concealing a flourishing case of chlamydia.

I stood there on his front steps, blinking, like a computer trying to process but coming up with the same error message. It didn't matter what I did, I couldn't make it work out. I couldn't get him back. Irritated that I wouldn't leave on my own accord, he slammed the door in my speechless face.

But where did his infection come from?

Did I just provide him with the perfect cover?

I couldn't decide which was worse: the possibility that I was the cause of all Michael's ills and the end of our relationship, or him creating all that unnecessary righteous drama to hide that he'd cheated on me too.

Since I didn't have the guts—or the confidence—to confront him about his own infidelity, I got back into my car and drove away.

I scolded God, the universe, dead relatives, and the laws of science for letting me down. There was no cosmic destiny at play here. The only person writing my romantic fate was me.

Great.

The road to cultural enlightenment and spiritual fulfillment that I thought would come from my epic solo trip abroad was paved instead with painful life lessons. As far as wisdom goes, beggars can't be choosers.

So I drove to Seth's place. I'd heard he'd been back a week. I wondered if he liked jazz.

CHAPTER 8

HEX AN EX

M y mother always said, "Never plan your life around a man."
Whoops.

Summer faded into fall. I enrolled in general studies at the University of Calgary and holed up in my mother's basement. This was not how I thought life would be after my "amazing trip abroad," but I was defeated. Michael hated me, and my other potential boyfriend, Seth, wanted to "just be friends" because I seemed "a little crazy right now." He moved away for college anyhow, so it didn't matter. The good news was that my hair grew back, and I wore it straight and long.

The latent STD Michael had accused me of carrying never materialized, so that remained an unsolved mystery. I spent my days basically stalking Michael, and this was before the Internet, so to stalk someone properly you needed a car. I trailed him from his house, to his classes, to the jazz club where he often played. I can only imagine what that bartender thought, serving me white wines night after night while I sat alone and silent at the bar, always leaving before Michael's band finished. I was a barfly in the making; I just didn't know how to tip well yet, so service was spotty. It was probably better that way; the less I drank the less likely I'd make a fool out of myself by calling out from the audience or *not* leaving when his set was over.

I wouldn't always be that wise when it came to bars and men.

AT SCHOOL, I didn't spend one lick of time in the humanities building getting to know my fellow classmates; instead, I'd hurry over to the music building while fixing my lipstick, hoping to run into Michael.

I relied on constant stimulation to distract me from analyzing my sad life. Going home at night was too depressing, so if I couldn't find Michael, I'd drive back to the university and hang out with a med student named Hal. I admired Hal so much because he possessed two qualities that I didn't: the ability to make goals that had nothing to do with Michael, and the discipline to see them through. He'd stay up all night studying, and I'd sit beside him attempting to absorb the words in my *Intro to Evolution* textbook, which must have read like pulp fiction next to his thick medical manuals.

During coffee breaks, I'd talk Hal's ear off about my damaged love life, and he'd advise me like an older brother by prescribing a reality check. He said that I needed to face facts and move on. Put science ahead of emotion. I understood perfectly well what he meant but was still secretly counting on Michael coming back to me.

By constantly loitering around the music building, pretending not to be waiting for Michael, I met Leo. Leo was a jazz pianist with long, stringy dirty-blond hair who was too skinny for his frame. He also smoked and drank too much. He was nothing like Michael, but he liked me, which I was slowly learning was "my type." Our connection was born out of proximity, driven by my desperate need to feel loved, and sustained by our mutual appreciation of this one Talk Talk album. Add a couple of six-packs and you're guaranteed some sloppy sex. Leo claimed he was too screwed up to get in a real relationship, and as far as I was concerned I was already in one, so that wasn't a problem for me.

My nightly schedule alternated between stalking Michael, drinking and sleeping with Leo, and studying with Hal. They were my Three Stooges. This pattern continued for months, well into midterms. In my *Primatology* textbook, I learned that I was pushing the limits of my "Dunbar number," or the maximum amount of people with whom one can maintain stable social relationships. Dunbar didn't know who he was dealing with.

I'm not sure if Michael caught wind of Leo, or if I was succeeding in slowly breaking him down, but all of a sudden he responded to my relentless coaxing and we wound up in bed, or rather back on the floor of his music studio. It was like winning the federal lottery, having all the money taken away by taxes, and then winning it back again on a scratch ticket. The next morning, I asked him if he wanted to meet me for lunch after my Sociology 101 lecture, but he said, "We're not getting back together."

Yeah, whatever. It would happen eventually.

But on the sixth or seventh time when Michael said, "Ophira, we're not getting back together," while buttoning up his jeans, it finally sank in.

I ran to Hal and told him through my tears that I had reached my limit and was going to move to another city to start all over again. Everything in Calgary reminded me of Michael, and the only cure was to strip my life of everything and create an entirely new one somewhere else. I was shocked when Hal said that sounded like a good idea for me. I trusted he was right. For the next month, I surgically removed myself from Calgary. I applied midsemester to McGill University in Montreal and was accepted. I packed up my stuff and called about a room in an apartment with a grad student and an artificial intelligence professor. Two days before New Year's Day, I flew two thousand miles across the country to Quebec and walked into a new gray cement humanities building, intending to lay down some roots. It was a ballsy move, and I didn't even tell Michael. It was too delicious to fantasize about how sorry he would be when he found out I was gone.

Yes, I'd heard that saying "You can run, but you can't hide." Fine, but you can still run.

Unfortunately, although I'd moved, I hadn't moved *on*. I'd altered every aspect of my surroundings, yet all I could do was obsess over Michael. The lack of familiarity reinforced my old bad habits, and I was so consumed with keeping his presence in my life, I titled all my journal entries "Dear Michael" and played silly mind games with life:

If the bus comes in two minutes, we'll get back together. Okay, three minutes. How about four minutes?

At night, I'd buy a sesame bagel fresh from the oven and eat it out front of the shop, which happened to be on my street (this ritual was arguably more satisfying than any relationship). With my eyes to the night sky, I'd ask the stars, "Does he notice that I'm gone? Does he miss me? What is he thinking? Is he hurting?" And because I really loved him, I really wanted him to hurt.

Once again, my only welcome distraction was Leo, who had also moved to Montreal—not to escape, but to be closer to his family. We continued our periodic friends-with-benefits situation (but it was before we knew that term, so it was called "I dunno") of guzzling cheap beer and waking up beside each other. Neither of us uttered a word about what was "going on," which made us fantastically compatible.

One afternoon, I was sitting on my red IKEA couch, pretending to read the ethnography *Yanomamo: The Fierce People* when my attention was actually on the phone, wondering if I could will it to ring. After an exhausting hour of inconclusive mind control, I convinced myself that there was no reason why *I* couldn't call Michael. People, friends, exes, check in with each other all the time. It's totally normal, not to mention courteous. Once I made the decision that I was allowed to call him, my mood lifted. I was happy for the first time in months.

Michael's cheerful "Hello?" set my heart cantering. This was back before caller ID, when people picked up the phone with excitement because they didn't know who or what might be waiting for them on the other end.

"Hi, Michael. It's Ophira!"

I heard a deep, audible sigh. "Oh. Hi, Ophira."

It was the equivalent of a party balloon deflating. I carried the momentum of our awkward chat, asking him all the standard questions about life and work, peppering the conversation with my own answers, since he wasn't asking. He'd heard that I'd moved but sounded totally indifferent about it. I could feel the unsatisfying conversation wind down, so in a last-ditch effort to make the call worth something, I asked the one question you're never supposed to ask an ex.

"Hey, Michael. I was wondering . . . are you seeing anyone?"

He replied effortlessly. "Yes, I am."

What? My insides twisted up. There was no way! He must be lying. How could he be seeing someone?

I weakly inquired, "Who?"

"Kimberly."

I'd seen Kimberly around the music department. She played the flute and was everything a flautist should be: waify, airy, blonde, and dumb. Actually, I didn't know if she was dumb or not; I just thought of her as the antithesis of me. It's flattering when the next person someone dates reminds people of you: he has brand loyalty; he just didn't like your particular model. However, it's a total insult when she's the polar opposite. That means he wants nothing to do with your company ever again. It seemed that I might have turned Michael against "Persistently Pining Acerbic Brunettes" forever.

There wasn't anything more to say, so we hung up. I thought of my anthropology book *Intro to Tribal Cultures*, feeling numb and jealous of all the brides captured in tribal wars. At least someone wanted them.

My new friends were so patient with me. They took me out and consoled me, reassuring me that I could do so much better while pointing out cute drunk guys that I should take advantage of on my rebound. One friend, Suzanne, who was particularly sick of my never-ending desperate ramblings, said in her thick Quebecois accent, "Why don't you go *visite de* Haitian witch doctor, no?"

Finally someone with some decent advice! She gave me the number, and I called to make an appointment with a woman named Natasha. The name threw off my confidence. Instead of conjuring the image of an exotic dark-skinned woman wearing necklaces made of bones, "Natasha" brought to mind the cartoon character from *Rocky and Bullwinkle:* the evil girlfriend with the heavy Russian accent and edgy haircut. Then again, as long as she could cast a spell, her name could be Scamarella, for all I cared.

On a cold, snowy Saturday afternoon, I knocked on the door of a suburban house, worried that I was being had. The house didn't look much like a witch doctor's abode, with its light-blue stucco and Hummel figurines peeking out of the window. *There had better be a basement,* I thought as the door opened. I envisioned walking into a room filled with heavy red drapes and low lighting, decked out with occult symbols, snarling taxidermy, and dripping candles. I also imagined that Natasha, despite her name, would at least be dressed like a gypsy. Instead, a very plain-looking woman in her thirties wearing a faded pink T-shirt and a pair of Gap jeans welcomed me in. Between voodoo appointments, she could have easily worked as a kindergarten teacher. At least she had a slight accent.

Natasha ushered me into a living room filled with shiny faux-mahogany furniture and a velvety green couch covered in plastic. I went to sit down, but she motioned to a small wooden chair instead. I guess I had to earn my spot on the good sofa. It didn't matter: I was sure I was getting scammed, but my skepticism suddenly morphed into a new, more hopeful idea: She doesn't need to hide behind mysterious razzle-dazzle because she *is* an authentic Haitian witch doctor. Still, a little extra black eyeliner would have been nice.

She clasped my hands in hers and asked very seriously, "What brings you here?" Talking to a Haitian witch doctor was like a therapy session, the difference being at the end she'd cast a hex! She studied my face as I blathered on about my love for Michael—how we dated and it was fireworks, endured a year apart, suffered a cataclysmic breakup, followed by me chasing him for another six months, and, finally, moving here. I wanted him back. She nodded like she'd heard it all before and said that for forty dollars I had a choice: I could cast a "Move On with Your Life" spell, or a "Come Back to Me" spell. Was she kidding? Without pause I said, "Come Back to Me."

She kept trying to sway me. "Are you sure?" she asked. "Because there's a special on the Move On with Your Life spell. I would recommend it for you." But I was dead set on Come Back to Me. There was no question. That's why I came.

Natasha gave me two green drugstore-quality candles and told me to mark each one off into seven sections. Every night at sunset for two weeks, I was to place one candle on his photo and burn a portion while reciting a passage of Haitian text that she'd written out phonetically on a card—much like the transliteration printed in a Passover Haggadah so you can sing along even if you don't know Hebrew.

I couldn't wait for sunset! I knew if my roommates caught me burning candles and reciting voodoo chants they would assume I'd made the leap from despair to insanity and raise my rent. I set up a makeshift altar in the depths of my closet, placing the candle on a photo of Michael playing guitar, and every night I entered into the dark arts and quietly performed my return-to-me ritual.

You might wonder if I was so far gone that I really thought this would work. I will say that performing my witchcraft prayer every night gave my life much-needed structure and meaning. It was grasping at straws, ridiculous, maybe a little stupid, but it was all I had. Not only did I think it would work—I was counting on it.

At the end of two weeks, I got out of bed with a huge smile on my face, drank some coffee, and skipped off to class. Every passing minute was part of a countdown to the season premiere of my life. As soon as I got home, I dropped my bag and coat on the floor and ran across the room to the phone. As I dialed, I felt clearheaded and healed.

"Hello?"

"Hi, Michael, it's Ophira."

And then it happened. Again.

Sigh. "Hi, Ophira."

I didn't hear angels singing or witches cackling; I heard the sound of a sad trombone go *wah wah*, followed by Natasha laughing. Nothing had changed. He was still dating that flautist, and the only one dumber than her was me for believing that some bullshit candle-burning could make Michael forgive me and fall back in love with me. It's not like Natasha had offered a money-back guarantee.

"Ophira?" Michael said.

I swallowed hard.

"Yes, Michael?"

"I think you should stop calling me for a while."

I searched for something to say. This was the opposite of what Natasha said would happen. This was not worth forty dollars. Maybe I didn't concentrate hard enough or said the wrong words. In a last-ditch attempt to get something out of the call, I said, "Okay, but promise me this: If by the time I'm thirty, we're both not married, you have to promise to give us another chance. Do you promise?"

It was hard to hear those pathetic words come out of my mouth, but I couldn't stop myself.

"Okay, Ophira, whatever," he muttered, and hung up.

Thirty years old seemed ancient to me. I had almost a decade to become the person he'd want back.

I was furious at Haiti and marched to my closet to throw away the remnants of my voodoo crap. I also threw out his photo, but then thought better of it, pulled it out of the trash can, and stuck it in the middle of a random book, hoping to forget which one. I wanted an immediate fix, someone to hold me, so I called Leo but he wasn't home. Instead, I walked down the street to the bagel store and ate a piping-hot poppy seed on the street, without even once looking up at the useless stars.

CHAPTER 9

THE TROUBLE WITH FIELDWORK

According to my anthropology texts, if you really want to understand another culture, you need to immerse yourself in it, and the surest way to do that is by sleeping with the indigenous population. It's called "doing fieldwork."

The textbook didn't exactly say that, but that was the approach I planned to take.

As I emerged from my smooth-jazz trance, I couldn't believe I'd almost thrown away my barely-legal years on one guitar-strumming man. I reembraced my original belief system that for women, love and marriage was a stealth attack on our potential to take over the world, and sex was the quickest way to get to know someone.

Combining my own philosophy with anthropological theory, I decided that going forward I'd approach love/romance/relationships with the detachment of a social scientist. Screw postmodernism; I was a postromantic. No longer would I succumb to the Eurocentric construct of a relationship. I wasn't looking for a boyfriend; I wanted an informant: someone I could sustain three months of a one-night stand with—at least enough time to try on his life, pick up a new skill, and get out before we got attached. It was like fostering rescue dogs. I also bought a black leather motorcycle cap and insisted on wearing it every day. I thought it made me look dangerous—the kind of person you wouldn't want to fuck with. In my mind, it also distinguished me from that weak, feeble girl who had loved and lost Michael.

I didn't know where to find "my people" at McGill, so I explored a few subcultures. Naturally I joined the college radio station again, and for the first few months I followed a motley crew of Goths and indie rockers to a variety of punk gigs. At a concert featuring an up-and-coming thrash-metal band, I looked in the graffitied mirror of the dive bar's filthy bathroom and admitted to my reflection that I hated both the scene and the music. I had filled my mosh-pit quota in life when I dated Tommy. I needed to move forward, not revisit adolescent angst. I kept the radio gig but ditched the scene in search of one that was more novel—at least to me.

McGill, nicknamed Harvard of the North by the students who went there, was the country's number one college at the time. It was so vastly superior to other Canadian universities that I didn't have the faintest clue what anyone was talking about in my lectures. While my classmates were engaging in discourse about Immanuel Kant, Michel Foucault, or Edward Said, I was offering up suggestions for lodging in exotic locales. Apparently, I'd had my nose buried in the equivalent of a bunch of Lonely Planet guides, while they'd spent their first semester reading philosophical treatises.

While zoning out in Anthro 202, unable to follow the professor, I spotted the first target of my flirty fieldwork project: Ryan Peeling. I could tell by the slight upward tilt of his chin that the culture I'd be infiltrating was "the society of old money." Old Anglo-Saxon money. He probably knew how to sail, golf, and charge a fancy dinner at the club to a house account.

We were definitely from different worlds.

I wanted a window into his lavish world—and not from the servant's quarters. I wanted to know what a winter tan felt like on my lips, what it was like to sip an aperitif with my bank manager. Although he wore the same Nirvana-inspired plaid button-down as the rest of us, I suspected he was more at ease in a sweater vest with a blue and green Izod tie poking out. As I watched him scribble down whatever the professor was saying, I noticed he was growing out a proper short haircut. I imagined his father was probably worried that his prized heir was going hippie on him. I'm sure the pursuit of an anthropology degree over a practical degree was disappointing enough.

When the next class began, I slid into the empty seat beside him—not that he noticed. He was too busy listening and raising his hand to ask intelligent questions. There was no way I could compete or impress on that level, so I tried to ingratiate myself by riffing off the lecture and mumbling little jokes and sarcastic lines: "Who wouldn't want to be a troglodyte? I bet they have cheap rent and dollar draft beers down there . . . must be nice to live in a mud hut. It never gets dirty! . . . The upside of bridal capture is that's a marriage that will probably last, and parents save a shitload on a wedding." I managed to coax one smirk out of him, which was a start, enough to say hi in the hallways.

I was casually persistent. Every time I saw Ryan sitting alone in our college lounge, "The Alley," I'd invite myself to join him. I'm not sure he knew what to make of this smiling, slightly aggressive new girl who was constantly demanding his attention, but he never asked me to leave. We progressed to going for coffee after class. While he told me all about his life, I drifted off into a fantasy. My brain had started doing this new trick I detested but couldn't control. I would listen to him while picturing us together in twenty years. Did other girls shamefully do this? Was it years of gender socializing, or were we hardwired to consider the nesting potential of whatever man held our current interest? There he was, likely undressing me in his head and imagining me bent over the hood of his car, while I was fantasizing about us tasting vintage wine at a Napa Valley inn. Naturally, my Ryan visions incorporated access to his wealth. First, he'd pay off my student loans. Next, I'd demand to dress only in difficult-to-even-dry-clean raw silk. He'd be some sort of academic researcher, constantly away at conferences, leaving room for me to tend our small-dog ranch and have an affair with my sculpture teacher in between conducting my own lecture series, "The Anthropology of Amour." Sure, it sounded more like a Learning Annex course, but I was still only a sophomore—I'd have plenty of time to revise my daydream.

After the Rituals and Shamanism lecture, Ryan and I were having our coffees when he said, "You know, I've never done any psychedelic drugs. I really want to try mushrooms, you know? Witness that shift in reality."

"Really? You've never done 'shrooms? What, was there actual shit to do in your town growing up?" I needled.

"No, well, we smoked pot," he said, trying to save face, "but no one in high school had anything else."

"Ha! Not that you know of!" And then an idea occurred to me. "I bet I can get us some 'shrooms," I said.

"How?" he asked eagerly.

"I . . . might know someone. Let me work on it, okay?"

He laughed at me. "Yeah, sure. You go work on that."

Not only had I dabbled in mushrooms numerous times and was well versed in what to expect, but I was also counting on the fact that if I helped him with his vision quest, things would progress beyond coffees.

If there was one thing I noticed about our campus, it was that the radio station was teeming with drug doers, sellers, and two-for-one deals. I walked in at lunch and very politely asked Louise, the programming assistant who was supposedly on methadone, if she knew where I could buy some mushrooms. Louise scared the shit out of me. It was clear she had no use for my big shiny face and bouncy demeanor, but she was happy to take my money. She handed me two tabs of acid and growled, "This is all I have. Ten dollars." Apparently, I didn't have a say in the matter, so I did as instructed and walked out with two squares of LSD in my purse. I wasn't crazy about doing acid again.

Now that I was twenty, I wanted to take care of my body and stick to the organics. But I wasn't about to argue this point with Louise.

I saw Ryan in The Alley reading *Das Kapital* and flopped across from him, eager to announce that I'd purchased the traditional opiate of the masses.

"So! If you're mad keen and wanna do acid tonight, I've *acquired* some," I said with a faux British accent, forgetting in that moment that I can't do accents. "It's pretty much like mushrooms but trippier." I was impressed with myself, proud of how spontaneous and savvy I seemed. I was no Betty Co-Ed; I was like Demi Moore in *St. Elmo's Fire*. And we all know how that ends. Eventually you sleep with Ashton Kutcher.

He said he was totally in, and we agreed to meet at the Double Deuce bar after class. I planned an outfit around my leather cap, adding bleached jeans, a purple velvet blazer, and chunky high boots. Unfortunately, I'd let myself get caught up in the excitement and overlooked one very important thing about acid: It doesn't make you touchy-feely or amorous at all. Heady and freaked out, sure, but it is the furthest thing from a sexy drug. We should have met up at the planetarium.

As the drug hit, Ryan went into philosophizing mode, relishing each word as it came out of his mouth like it was a hunk of conversational caramel.

"If Nietzsche was right and there's no such thing as *truth*, because my truth is different from your truth, then this is one kind of beer to me, but it's completely something else to you. Think about it."

I nodded, but I'd started the trip with a specific goal in mind, and the effects of the acid only cemented my purpose and made it more urgent.

"There is no such thing as objectivity," he continued. "We can never be anything but subjective. Ever." He looked at me. Even with a strong chemical moving through my bloodstream, I wasn't that interested in this discussion. Ryan continued on an intellectual rampage about how anthropological writing was about as useful as literary criticism, while I fixated on the task of how I was going to get him to kiss me. At that moment, I didn't desire for him to kiss me, I just needed it, like it was an item on a scavenger hunt. Locking lips with him would also have the side benefit of shutting him up.

Before our third beer, I lied and said, "All these people are kinda wigging me out. Do you wanna walk back to my place? It's closer than yours." His eyes were two huge black pupils that seemed to spiral into outer space.

"Totally," he replied. Then he said my face had a pretty neon outline around it. *Your face is pretty* would have worked for me, but we were getting closer.

In my sparse white bedroom, decorated only with a couple of postcards and one two-dollar deli plant, we lay propped up on pillows on my futon, listening to Tom Waits. Ryan was . . . still talking. He wanted to review the history of civilization in the confines of my room, starting with Greco-Roman times, and I wanted to reenact a Bacchanalian ritual. I edged over ever so slightly so our thighs were touching, hoping that if our bodies came close enough together, magnetic forces would take over. I felt nothing. I couldn't sense any flirty vibes coming off him, and with the acid, you'd think I'd actually be able to *see* them. As he continued with his commentary, now about how eyesight is the most complex example of cellular division, it struck me that he might not be that into *me* because he was too into himself. I was a mere prop in his solo trip.

Eventually the drug started to wear off, and our eyes flickered with fatigue. It was 1:00 AM, and one thing was clear through my fading LSD-tinted contacts: It wasn't going to happen with Ryan. He was a stubborn and loquacious research subject. Our parched lips briefly touched before he left, the kind of kiss you get from a confused third cousin. This fieldwork was going to be more challenging than I'd anticipated . . . and soon I'd need to apply for a research grant. Ryan never gave me the five bucks for his portion of the acid. My mother would say, "That's how the rich stay rich."

Back in anthropology class, I spent the entire lecture intently studying every other single male specimen in the class, sizing them up, ranking them, and mentally pie-graphing the results like I did back in Cheryl's basement. In my kinship chart, I narrowed down the criteria to two categories: my general interest and percentage chance of it actually happening. I needed to cut my teeth on some surer bets. My top two prospects: the supernerdy redhead Kieran, because he looked like the male version of the sexy librarian and might be a vivacious animal under that maroon cardigan; and the mildly exotic Ramon, a Middle Eastern–looking boy with a bumpy nose who spoke perfect Quebecois French. I'd pursue them in that order of difficulty. Screw waiting around to get roofied at an Omega-Delta-Who-Cares keg party; I was handpicking my fraternity.

I got Kieran into bed immediately. It was almost too easy, and he was too thrilled and too thankful, like I'd granted his Make-A-Wish. I surely wasn't his first, but I was one of four. His inexperienced hands almost shook as they touched me, and the sex itself remained in its earliest stage of development: very perfunctory with virtually nothing in it for me. All I got was a mild workout. I waved good-bye while he was still in bed, dazed in his tighty-whities, and bought myself a coffee on my way home so I could get some postcoital studying done. Nothing is a bigger turnoff than someone who is overly grateful. *Blech.*

Next, I asked Ramon out for a drink. He complimented my leather cap, and I invited myself back to his apartment. Things went so much faster and smoother when I took charge of the date. Ramon turned out to be so nice that I wanted to go out with him just to see if I could make him angry. If he were in a tribe, it would be with the levelheaded hunters. He was also some sort of genius who'd already obtained a computer science degree and had returned to school to get an anthropology degree, for fun! If his idea of a good time was getting a second bachelor of arts, I was about to show him another dimension. He also owned a business—some spacey company that made lasers or photons or luncheon meat or something.

Ramon didn't have any roommates, but he certainly knew how to entertain. Once we were in his place he swiftly moved us from a glass of wine in his kitchen to something a little stronger in his bedroom. What a relief it was to be with someone experienced. There was no discussion and no anxiety emanating from his body. Plus, he was such a good student that I stopped paying attention in class. While we cuddled after sex, I'd ask him to summarize our shared lectures. It was like sleeping with Cliff of CliffsNotes. I dragged him to bars and parties, and once even persuaded him to do ecstasy with me. Occasionally he'd complain that since he'd met me he wasn't getting any work done. I took it as a compliment and asked him to massage my feet because my heels were killing me.

Dying to get a taste of the real Montreal, I kept pestering him to introduce me to his family. We could go together to the famous Cheval Blanc bar; they could teach me how to make *poutine* (a true delight of French fries, gravy, and partially melted cheese curds), and how to curse the Anglos. Then Ramon invited his mother and me over for dinner. His mother worked professionally as a fortune-teller and astrologer. (Was everyone in Montreal connected to the dark arts?) I was pretty sure Ramon was supplementing her income and there was pressure on him to become the family's replacement breadwinner. Returning to college to take an anthropology degree was his subtle way of rebelling.

I sensed by the way she shook my hand that she already didn't like me. After reviewing how to properly pronounce my name, she asked, "What's your sign, sweetie?"

"Capricorn!" I said proudly.

She smiled like she had a secret. I wondered if she knew Natasha.

"You're a Capricorn. That's nice. Strong-minded, a dry sense of humor, a late bloomer."

Was she or my Zodiac sign insulting me?

"You know, Ramon is a Libra. Capricorns and Libras . . . " She wagged her index finger back and forth. "It doesn't work. The man likes balance. A goat can never give him that." And then she glanced over at Ramon, who was making her a coffee.

I don't know if there's a French term for being told your future against your will, but I bet the Germans have a word for it. According to the stars, I was a clumsy animal that shouldn't be allowed anywhere near a double-beam scale. I tried not to take what she said too literally, but I was alone in that. Ramon broke up with me a week later. He argued that I was sucking him dry, and that his company and schoolwork were suffering. I couldn't deny that I took up a lot of his time, but it wasn't my fault that he couldn't keep up. He said that I didn't need a boyfriend—I needed a tutor and a masseuse. Clearly he needed an Aquarius or a Virgo, or whatever sign doesn't value fun. We both know what his mother really meant to say: "Get the hell away from my son, slut; you'll never be one of us," or as the French say, *"À bientôt!"*

Well, *va te faire foutre* to you.

Everything sounds better in French.

MY FINAL FIELDWORK project came in my senior year. The catalyst was an old friend, Carol, who came to live with me after McGill hired her as its theater director in residence. We knew each other from working at a café back in Calgary and became fast friends once we discovered that beer foam looked like steamed milk if you poured your Molson into a café au lait bowl fast enough. Being around Carol was like being at an ongoing theater festival. She had a joyful laugh that she used liberally (making her the best audience member ever) and was the only woman I'd ever met who'd decoupage things and they'd actually look better. My roommates were immediately enchanted by her aura, and they agreed to throw a mattress in the middle of our living room for six months in exchange for a little rent money.

On her second night, while I prepared us a dinner of tofu and beans (I was a vegetarian back then because I didn't know how to safely handle meat) and she constructed a modern art mobile, she asked if she could invite over her friend Sammy who was taking drama at Concordia, "the other university." I didn't know anyone studying at the *other*, more artsy university. It was like entertaining a Montague. Of course I said yes, and I was glad I did. Sammy turned out to be so adorable. He was a hipster before we knew what they were, striking the perfect balance between skateboarder and philosophy professor by pairing sneakers and an old concert T-shirt with tortoiseshell glasses and a full beard. His curly mahogany hair framed his face in such a way that he looked like a handsome version of the cowardly lion from *The Wizard of Oz*. He also lived in a headspace similar to Emerald City. It was all theater and puppets, masks and make-believe. His joie de vivre was infectious. I felt lighter around him. We all laughed recalling our favorite Muppet Movie moments, and when it was time for him to leave, I offered to walk him halfway home, pretending I needed to stop by the corner store to get some orange juice for the morning. Carol gave me a wink as I struggled to put on my winter boots.

Sammy and I kicked snow around on Parc Avenue, discussing how beautiful Montreal was in comparison with prefab Calgary, where he, too, had grown up.

"And have you ever seen so many amazing churches?" I said, stopping in front of a beautiful sandstone church with a carved steeple that happened to be right on the street. We stood in silence, staring at the ornate gargoyles and carvings, two Jews fascinated with the exquisiteness of a Christian house of worship.

"Maybe they left one of the doors open by accident," I said, running up the stone steps.

"No church leaves its doors unlocked at midnight, Ophira," Sammy said, as I tugged on the handles and one of the heavy wooden doors released and swung open. I looked back at him with a massive grin. I had this one.

The cathedral was pitch black except for dozens of red vigil lights at the front illuminating a statue of Mary. It was part eerie and part unbelievably seductive. Suddenly it became very clear to me what needed to happen next. When two single Jewish college students are alone in a church at night, it is mandatory that they get it on. I believe it's written in the Torah. In the middle aisle, halfway to the pulpit, we started necking in front of holy Jesus on the cross. I wanted to take things a step further; when would *this* happen again? But Sammy insisted that we had pushed the donations envelope far enough. It was too risky and a little disrespectful. I didn't want to piss him off, or the Lord, really, since he was so cool about leaving the door unlocked, so I backed down, and we reluctantly parted ways, with flushed cheeks and red noses. I needed to see more of this guy.

We held off from sleeping together for a while. Two days. Hanging out with Sammy was like entering into a children's book. He asked me if I wanted to help out on opening night of his school's production of *A Midsummer Night's Dream*, which involved getting dressed up as sprites and handing out beverages or hanging coats. Of course! We were both ecstatic about the invitation to get costumed. Sammy and I were a perfect match in the woodland fairy world, and we had the best sex of our six-month relationship while dressed as pixies, our silver and green eye shadow and lipstick mixing together. If we were going to role-play, it would be Elizabethan-themed and involve iambic pentameter.

Unfortunately we were mere mortals, not flying nymphs, and much like the acid and the ecstasy, Puck's spell soon wore off, too. My pragmatic nature wore on him, and his whimsical demeanor frustrated me. Occasionally I wanted to commiserate about how little money I had, how much my roommates were bothering me, or how I was struggling with whatever the hell I was doing with my life without Sammy breaking into song, cueing the marionettes, or denying it by entering the world of make-believe. Like actors after closing night, we had no way of relating to each other once thrust into the real world. During final exams, which were always a torturously tough time for me, Sammy suddenly flew home to be with his family. I was furious and told him that he was like everyone else (meaning Michael), abandoning me when times got tough. He replied that the only common denominator in that equation was me.

I liked him better with the puppets.

Fieldwork was unpredictably hard, and informants were demanding and high maintenance. It was also impossible for me not to get a little emotionally attached. Sammy and I broke up over the phone during finals, a long-distance call that I paid for. With a month left in college, I got drunk at a party and made out with my best friend, Rebecca, to make sure I'd checked off that box and fulfilled my college duties. Her mouth was too small and too soft. It was like kissing a Precious Moments doll.

Having never learned enough French to be able to get a job in Montreal, and with no obvious application for my cultural anthropology degree other than sleeping around, I decided to move again, this time to Vancouver, where my older sister had offered me a free bed. I did, however, learn to understand a little Michel Foucault and even printed up a quote of his and pasted it above my Macintosh Classic for inspiration: "I don't feel that it is necessary to know exactly what I am. The main interest in life and work is to become someone else that you were not in the beginning."

I suspected that I was on that path, even after I donated my black leather biker cap to the radio station.

CHAPTER 10

UNSEND

Everyone loves Vancouver: You can ski in the morning, windsurf in the afternoon, and smoke your buddy's top-shelf hydroponic pot at night. It was the perfect place to be if you had no solid plans. No one cared if you had your shit together, were working toward a career, or were a productive member of society. As long as you recycled and were nice to animals, you were, as we Canadians say, eh-okay. So why wasn't I drawn to a city whose motto is "By Sea, Land, and Air We Prosper"? Because I prospered in dark basements. I didn't care about hiking or jumping off a cliff. My idea of an endorphin spike was persuading the cute guy at the end of the bar to come home with me.

I had no reason to hold a grudge against the place. Pivotal moments in my early sexual history took place in "The 'Couv." The first was at sixteen when my oldest sister dressed me and my three best friends up in her spandex nightclubbing clothes, teased our hair, and took us to see Chippendale dancers. Her attitude was that if we were going to drink underage, it might as well be on her watch, thus making her the coolest sister ever. I think she found us highly entertaining, the way we strutted around in high heels and fake lashes, pretending we were grown up and could handle our liquor, as if we were auditioning for *Teens and Tiaras*.

We may have had some experience with booze, but none of us had ever seen live adult men naked before. That Chippendale performance stuck with me over the years because it was so . . . creepy. The guys were more intimidating than titillating. They seemed too confident, too *into* their jobs as strippers, screwing up the whole power dynamic. I would have liked more sensitive men, guys who were broken down, vulnerable, and ashamed to be exotic dancers. If any of them had shed an embarrassed tear during his dance, I would have given him a twenty. Plus, I didn't relate to their ridiculous job-related Halloween costumes: the doctor, the policeman, the fireman. Where was the professor, the bike courier, the barista? The headliner was the worst: a greased-up man in a ponytail and a leopard-print bikini yelling, "Me Tarzan! You Jane!" The poor guy actually placed a CorningWare casserole pot on stage filled with kerosene, lit it, and then seductively danced around and over his tiny campfire. All I could think was—would he use that later to make scalloped potatoes? Was that the smell of burning hair?

Two years later at eighteen, I spent a week on the beach in Vancouver with my new best friend from ballet, Michelle, listening to a single Violent Femmes CD and fooling around with random guys. Actually, I don't think Michelle ever touched any of them. She was by far the prettier one and was saving herself either for marriage or at least for someone truly worth it. Not me. I was out there getting fingered in the ocean, which was about as orgasmic as watching a guy thrust his junk over a flaming CorningWare pot. I couldn't wait to be old enough to have my own place where I could lie down.

DURING MY FIRST few months crashing at my sister Avigail's place, I did absolutely nothing. I didn't have a job or a schedule. I'm not even sure I brushed my teeth every day. At month five it became clear, by way of a sisterly ultimatum, that I needed to find my own place and make some money. The job came easy. It was at a business where I'd pictured myself working for many years: Kinkos. Sure, Montreal had *poutine,* smoked meat, and a great sense of style, but did it have a Kinkos? No. How was a college student like myself expected to get any major projects done if I couldn't photocopy a book or print a paper after hours? Who did homework before midnight? It was a constant frustration. Then I moved to Vancouver and saw it in big glossy blue letters: Kinkos. I would have called mine ProcrastaPrint or something else more obviously fitting than a made-up word that sounded like a fetish club for clowns.

Impressed by my knowledge of Microsoft Word, Kinkos hired me on the spot and put me in charge of renting out computers by the minute and helping people with their word processing problems. The other computer employees, distinct from the copy people, were geeky boys still struggling with acne, twenty-sided dice, and what to say to girls. They were great when I needed to pawn off an unwanted shift, but that's where the courtship ended. I needed someone more my speed. It was slim pickings on the copier side too. Let's just say that Kinkos didn't employ any handsome Fulbright scholars—it was the sort of job that attracted lost souls, extreme potheads, and me. I was delighted to discover that if you heard "safety meeting" announced over the PA system, it meant someone was about to spark up a joint in the back alley. Safety meetings took place multiple times a day. The regular customers must have thought that handling toner was extremely dangerous.

I fell into a convenient, one-sided flirtation with a very tall, very thin, half-hippie half-just-broke dude named Bruce. He had the most amazing green eyes and Mick Jagger lips, if only he'd cut his stringy shoulder-length hair to show them off. Although he had decent hygiene, he never quite looked clean, as if he were perpetually covered in a layer of dust. At the same time, he was one of those people obsessed with offbeat health fads and was currently drinking two cups of olive oil a day. Maybe that was why the dirt stuck to him. He doted on me with everything he had to offer, and as the rides home, the free beers, and the bummed cigarettes added up, I could tell he was getting impatient, wondering when we'd take things to the next level. The only thing climaxing for me was my guilt. I didn't want to lose him as a loyal companion. I also didn't have the faintest clue why he liked me so much.

It may have been a special occasion like his birthday or something that intensified my shame level, but I finally gave in and slept with him. I don't remember the quality of the sex because I was drunk and high (big surprise), but I do remember how fat and round I felt next to his long, thin body. He was like a cricket, all elbows and knees knocking together. After, while he was getting me a glass of water and himself a cup of oil, I actually asked him, "Hey, why do you like me?"

"*Duh,*" he answered back. "Cuz you're awesome." It was nice to be awesome but it was not specific enough of an answer for me to draw any solid conclusions. I tried to avoid him after my bed surrender as I had no intention of duplicating that evening, and I didn't want to have to be faced with telling him that. I needed to find a new job since it was becoming increasingly clear that I was in the top 1 percent of awesome at Kinkos. And when you hit the glass ceiling at the copy shop, it's time to move on, at least to a Starbucks.

While still working there, pondering who I was and what I was doing with my life, I tried stand-up comedy. It altered me chemically forever.

There is a correlation between me and sex, and me and stand-up. There's the obvious therapy angle—the bottomless well of self-loathing that no amount of adoration by strangers will ever fill, *blah blah blah*. Boring. The more visceral link between the two has to do with the deep connection you create with a person when you have sex and with a crowd when you get a laugh. Even if you can bond for a brief second, it's a moment of bliss, a wave of pure release. Good sex that is. I would seriously rather do the worst stand-up show than have bad sex, any day.

I'd been secretly flirting with the idea of trying stand-up for years but didn't know where to start. The most proactive, yet safe, thing I could think to do was volunteer as an usher for a comedy festival. It ended up being a good choice. A few of the other ushers were actual up-and-coming stand-ups, and after we shined flashlights in one another's faces for ten minutes, they invited me to come check out a workshop for wannabe comedians. I guffawed at the idea. You can't teach funny in a class. Yet I found myself signing up, with the intention of skipping out after the first hour, before they collected their money. Nice try. This outfit knew what they were doing and asked for the money at the door. I hemmed and hawed, then found myself taking out $300 from the ATM, still suspicious that I was being roped into a scam and being sold a lofty dream. In a way, I was.

In front of ten other hopeful amateur comics, I told a few stories, little anecdotes that I'd used over the years to try to amuse my friends. The teacher said he saw talent in me and suggested I do the "graduation show"—the next night. I couldn't believe a weekend workshop had a graduation show. But those were the words I'd waited to hear my entire life, and it only cost me three hundred bucks! The following night I called in sick for my shift at Kinkos and stepped out onto the stage for the first time.

To be clear, I wasn't anything special, just another person trying stand-up for the first time, so, pretty terrible. I believe my opening line was, "So my name is Ophira. People always ask me, what kind of name is that? And I tell them it's Hebrew. I'm from the land of Heeb." I heard *a* laugh, resulting in the biggest rush of my life. It was like jumping out of a plane while having sex with the guy people told Clive Owen he looked like. But I was paralyzed by the idea of actually *pursuing* stand-up comedy. The whole thing was so daunting. My family would never approve of my hanging out in bars all night, making no money, and dealing with drunk people. Then again, that was almost exactly what I did already. But there was also dying miserably in front of a crowd or having a heckler ruin you—it seemed too much for me to bear. The comedy teacher did nothing to assuage that fear. He warned, "When you die onstage, you die alone."

So you could say that I was afraid of the truth.

On the advice of the stand-up teacher, I signed up for an acting class; it was a garden party by comparison. Not that I was a naturally good actor either, but the atmosphere was nurturing. The class was all about having faith in yourself and your scene partner, and everyone hugged at the end. One of my acting-class partners, Cindy, begged me to go out with her friend Phillip, claiming he was the "best guy ever." Never believe a single girl who says she has the greatest single guy for you. If he's so amazing, why isn't she with him? I took her endorsement to heart after letting her slap my face in a trust exercise and agreed to have coffee with him. He insisted we meet at a "nonchain café," as he referred to it, which I appreciated.

I looked over this "best guy ever." He resembled Tom Wopat, Luke from *The Dukes of Hazzard* (or Johnny Knoxville, depending on your generation) but with a massive Jew fro. So like a Heeb of Hazzard. I could definitely work with it.

We both ordered a regular coffee with milk, no bullshit. The barista rang us up for $2.50.

"Do you need some money?" I offered, after watching him search through his wallet for many minutes.

He looked confused and then gestured for me to speak into his other ear. "I blew this ear out listening to Beethoven too loud when I was sick in bed," he said.

What did that even mean? Regardless, he had my attention, and I had to know more.

"Do you need some money for the coffees?" I yelled into his other ear.

"No, I got it, but this is weird," he said, delicately holding up a tiny piece of paper. "I found a couple tabs of acid in my wallet. I guess I forgot about them. I have no idea how long they've been there. Do you think acid expires?"

What was it with me and acid?

"I guess we should find out, right?" I said into his good ear.

I can't say I was convinced that he'd conveniently found two tabs of acid in his wallet, but I applauded the fact that he'd prepared a pitch. I was more than happy to follow along.

He handed me my tiny square of paper.

"I never thought I'd do acid again," he lied.

"Me neither!" I lied.

And with that, we each swallowed a mouthful of LSD-laced java.

"It's so nice out. Should we walk?" he suggested. There is nothing more attractive than a man with a plan.

We sauntered along the shoreline, high out of our heads, for about twelve hours. By the time we made it to breakfast, I was too worn out to think about the logistics of making sex happen, let alone a shower and a nap. He really did blow out his ear while sick with the flu when he was fifteen; he put the speaker right near his bed, dialed the volume up to ten, and basically hugged it while listening to Beethoven. He ended up closer to Ludwig than he'd bargained for. But I liked this guy. He was a complete anomaly.

We parted after pancakes and shared a quick, syrupy kiss. I worried that I whispered my number into his bad ear. We hung out two more times. The sex was surprisingly straightforward for a guy who stuffed drugs in his wallet and punctured his eardrum listening to a symphony. Not that I was waiting for an invitation to swing from the rafters, but I thought he'd amaze me with some real passion. He was the first person I'd ever been with who smoked a cigarette after sex, and he was surprised I'd never tried it. He claimed, "Because of the chemicals and the endorphins surging through your body, it tastes totally amazing." He was right; it tasted more sugary, almost like cherries. That's when I realized chemicals were this guy's "thing."

The Zagat review for Phillip would say that although he was "unique," he wasn't much for "hanging out in public spaces" as they were "too unpredictable." All he wanted to do was blow cherry-laced smoke circles in bed. The third time I called to try to convince him to come out for drinks with my friends, he didn't return my call. Perhaps he didn't hear his phone ring. I have no idea what happened to him. My guess is that he replenished his wallet with another couple of tabs of acid for the next girl. It's what made him the "best guy ever."

Through a friend of a friend, I landed both a house-sitting gig and a job as a receptionist at a sewage pump company. Shit was about to start paying my bills. I was the world's worst receptionist: I came in late every day and could never figure out how to transfer calls and play Minesweeper at the same time. The environment was stale, serious, and cold. Actually freezing. The office complex was so overair-conditioned I took to wearing layered turtlenecks and arm warmers in the middle of August. I was the only single girl in the office, with the exception of the head secretary, who admitted that late at night she talked to angels. Not one angel. Many.

I was beyond lonely, and house-sitting was starting to get to me. Staying alone in a strange apartment full of someone else's stuff—their snow globes, beaded pillows, and framed photos of smiling people having a good time at weddings and barbecues—can make you feel invisible. Sometimes I'd pretend I was there; I was the one taking the photo, getting everyone to smile. I began to understand why people talked to angels.

The only imprint I was leaving in life was that of my butt on the couch. I knew every crack in the ceiling and every fleck of peeling paint on the door frames from studying them intensely while lying on my back. I wasn't sure how to move forward, so I started reflecting on the past, remembering happier times when I'd felt valued, had a purpose—like back in Montreal. I started to glamorize my college years as if they were a golden era, discarding all the difficult stuff: the panic of not getting papers done, the stressful exams, the weird cliques, and the confusing relationships. Suddenly, my college years were the best years of my little life.

I also romanticized Sammy. I missed him, mostly because . . . he was the last guy I really dated. I forgot all about our inability to connect emotionally unless it was through masks and puppets, and reminisced instead about our *Midsummer Night's* sex, his dreamy sense of wonder, drinking cheap wine, and laughing. We did do that, right? I couldn't quite remember, but I was pretty sure that we were borderline soul mates. So I called him. I was sitting on the couch, bored. I didn't even let my brain debate whether it was a good idea or not; I just picked up the phone and dialed his number.

We talked. It flowed easily, and I was surprised at how happy he was to hear from me. We entertained each other with witty observations about our twentysomething lives. He told me about his recent adventure smoking a little pot and syncing up Pink Floyd's *The Dark Side of the Moon* with *The Wizard of Oz* movie, which I'd never heard of anyone doing before. Sounded supercool. I felt as if we were totally on the same wavelength. I wasn't even annoyed when he slipped into little cartoon character voices or told me about some Irish poetry he was really getting into. If anything, my past relationship amnesia was only getting worse. The nostalgia made our connection feel deeper. I was tormented by the feelings erupting in me, and now I couldn't recall why we'd broken up in the first place. Before we hung up he said, "Let's talk again."

I mulled it over for a week and asked the universe for guidance. On my way to work in the morning, I'd say things in my head like, *Okay world, if Sammy and I aren't meant to be together again then someone on this bus should ask for my phone number.* I was asked if I needed a transfer, had change for a dollar, and to move out of the way, but that was it. So I was confident that we were meant to be. It was that simple.

One night I came home from the shit factory clutching a bottle of Merlot and a Lean Cuisine dinner. I tore off my wool turtleneck, poured a mug of wine, and quickly became maudlin. It was time to call Sammy and lay it all on the line. I picked up the phone and then slowly replaced it on the receiver. Had I come to my senses? No. I'd hatched an even better plan. I'd write him a letter. That way I'd have uninterrupted time to tell him how I really felt, without the fear of getting shot down midpitch. I was going to be honest. And we all know that when it comes to mixing Merlot with ex-boyfriends, honesty's the worst policy.

I scribbled that letter quickly, and by the end it was five pages of flowery prose describing my longing, mixed in with apologetic please-take-me-back drivel. I used the kind of language you'd read in a romance novel to describe how I felt about him, like *rapturous, lavish, pulsing, heaving,* and *hot.* It was more of an open letter to my imaginary, ideal man than to Sammy, but I signed it, folded it, and searched for an envelope as if I were running a race. I knew I had a small window of time before I sobered up and talked myself out of the whole thing. Rummaging through a desk, I found a stamp but didn't see an envelope anywhere. I was on the verge of ransacking the place when I realized I could make an envelope by folding a piece of paper in half and taping up the edges. As a matter of fact, it looked so good that I thought, *I'll never have to buy envelopes again. Think of all the money I'll save!* I ran out in search of a mailbox at ten thirty at night.

The second I heard the scraping metal sound of the mail chute slamming shut instead of a rush of relief I was filled with dread. *What*

did I just do? Nooooo! I didn't want to be with an up-and-coming pup-
peteer. All the real memories flooded back in HD: the despondent
looks across the breakfast table, his surprising me on Valentine's Day
by inviting his friend Jason to join us for dinner, the fact that on a very
basic level, I didn't *really* get him, nor did he *really* get me. We had such
a good conversation over the phone only because I wasn't talking with
anyone these days. He had zero competition.

If you think you can't unsend an e-mail, try getting a letter out of
a mailbox. Impossible. I had no choice but to return home and finish
the Merlot.

Another week passed. I picked up the phone one evening to hear
Sammy's voice. We muddled through hellos and how-are-yous, and
then he blurted out, "I should tell you that I got engaged. You don't
know her, but we met a few months ago."

Wow. That was not what I'd expected to hear. I felt even more
rejected. Sammy, on the other hand, must have felt great. As far as he
was concerned, everyone wanted him.

"So, I got your letter," he continued.

"I'm sorry." It was all I could muster.

I took a breath and prepared to tell him that I was drunk or high
or both and missing him, and it was a dumb thing to do. Before I could
get out my opening line, Sammy laughed.

"So now you're making your own envelopes?"

"Yeah, I'm trying to save money. No, I couldn't find one so I
thought I'd just make one . . . "

"Well, you're not very good at it."

Sammy went on to explain that he received my letter—sort of. He had received my homemade envelope, but that was all. It seemed that the Dollar Store scotch tape wasn't quite up to snuff, and the envelope snapped open somewhere along its mail journey causing the letter to drop out.

I couldn't believe it. It was a mail miracle. I was saved. This was amazing. There must have been an angel watching over me.

"So, *um*, what was the letter about? Why are you sorry?" he asked.

"Nothing, no reason. I felt bad for calling you out of the blue, and I thought I'd write you, you know, like people would write people when we were kids. I just like letters." Now I was feigning nostalgia for the lost world of pen pals. "But that's great about the engagement. Best of luck!"

We said our good-byes. This time we meant it.

I didn't even care if Sammy was lying. At least he came with a plan.

CHAPTER 11

LEGALLY BLIND

The longer I lived in Vancouver, the more depressed I got. Even worse, I was at peace with my sadness. I wasn't going anywhere, and I wasn't worried about it. There was a morose coziness to the place. Once you accepted the nine months of rainy gray skies, they wrapped around you like a lukewarm blanket. I couldn't decide if it was heaven disguised as a city, or a moss-covered jail. My only real responsibility was keeping track of an umbrella.

Every so often I'd have enough guts to sign up for amateur night, and if I got on stage, all I wanted was reassurance that I was funny. However, the general response afterward was that I was "very brave" or "seemed very smart." It was like telling an ugly person, "Hey, it's great how your face is . . . always there, and your eyes really know how to blink." I'd return home to the apartment I shared with a prison guard and her misanthropic landscaper brother who was the meanest gardener I'd ever met. If I'd had any real courage, I would have sat him down and said, "Listen, if you hate flowers that much, quit. It's okay. Maybe your sister can get you a nice job at a jail before you otherwise end up there."

Meanwhile, I found some seasonal employment as an income tax return sorter for Taxation Canada. It had all the classic markings of a true soul-sucking job: a draining forty-five-minute commute to an industrial suburb of brown government buildings, a windowless basement office with rows of identical cramped cubicles, and an ID badge with an unflattering, out-of-focus photo. Fifty other people and I would open up tax returns, put the forms in order, mark down if something was missing, and then separate them into piles. It paid a decent hourly wage with bonuses for speed. The fastest person was a woman in her mid-sixties who averaged around 170 tax returns an hour. I never broke one hundred.

I loved that job.

There was something about its simplicity, its mindlessness, that appealed to me at the time. There would be no upward mobility, no promotions, and no reason to settle in. I never made friends with any of my coworkers, nor did they attempt to learn my name. We'd arrive, sit in our cubicles, sort papers, and leave. One perk was that we were permitted to listen to music while we worked. I opted to borrow the entire Kurt Vonnegut collection of books on tape from the library, thinking I would have deeper insight into his characters if I listened to them while working for the man in the tan suit.

In between rewinding *Breakfast of Champions* and stapling

forms, I hung out at Gene's apartment. I'd met Gene through the comedy scene. He was a radio DJ who was legally blind and legally albino, meaning that he couldn't drive and had to avoid the sun. His hair was three shades lighter than wheat, and the lenses of his glasses were so thick they magnified his eyes, making him look like a Manga character. We got along famously. He had a razorsharp wit, loved shock humor, and was very, very funny—all personality traits expertly honed to compensate for his odd looks. Gene and I would spend hours smoking pot and bantering, volleying jokes and comments back and forth until the sun came up. Good talk is like seduction, and although I never felt any sexual vibe off him, he'd always comment that I was the most beautiful woman he'd ever met. Then again he was legally blind.

It was another typical night of hanging out. We were only about three joints in, laughing along to Jerky Boys tapes, when Gene put his arm around me, as if we were on a first date. I saw it coming, much like how once I looked at my sideview mirror and watched a car rear-end me. I didn't try to stop him; I went for the ride, mostly out of curiosity. We kissed, stopped to nonverbally check in with each other, and mutually returned a "Yeah, why not?" shrug. At worst, we'd be able to laugh about it later, right? He probably had *something* cool to show me. As we moved into his bedroom, Gene pinned my arms against the wallpapered hallway and said, "I'm warning you, you're about to see the smallest penis ever."

Talk about managing expectations. I replied in my usual upbeat manner, "I'm sure it's fine."

Our bedroom compatibility didn't hold a candle to the intimacy we shared sitting fully clothed across the room from each other. There was no artistry to what we were doing; it was like we both wanted to get it over with. I did everything I could to not look down at his penis, afraid that the resulting expression on my face would damage him forever. Then again, it's not like he could see it. In spite of this, it was the only time in my life I had to ask, "Are you sure it's in?" I'd never understood how or why anyone would have to ask that, but all of a sudden I was honestly inquiring.

He claimed, *"Yes, it's in,"* and I suspected that further investigation wouldn't help things.

Suddenly he announced that he was "done" and left the half-made bed to throw out the condom, which was weird because I didn't remember seeing him put one on. Was he wearing it the whole night in anticipation? I quickly got dressed and called out that I was going to grab a cab. He yelled, "See you later, sucker," from the bathroom, and then I heard water running. I hoped we didn't just fuck everything up.

He didn't contact me that week, and I finally broke down on Sunday and called him to assess the damage. We chatted like nothing had happened, which was a huge relief, but he also announced that he was moving to Ottawa for a while, or maybe it was Toronto, for some radio training, or a job, or family stuff, I can't remember which. It didn't matter; all I heard was that he was leaving, and I was sure it had everything to do with whatever that was we'd done together. Thinking back, it was a little presumptuous to assume that my actions profoundly affected his life, travel plans, and career path, but the timing was too perfect. I feared that I was losing my best friend.

Before he hung up, Gene mentioned that his pal was going through a hard time and could use someone fun to hang out with. I should give him a call. Flattered that he considered me the go-to person for cheering up, I told him I'd be happy to do some outreach work on his behalf. At the very least I could use this friend to maintain a connection to Gene.

On the phone, Roger sounded a little dull. Not boring, but not very quick. Nothing like Gene. He asked me to meet him for a cappuccino over the weekend. It seemed harmless enough, so I said sure.

We met at an Italian café on Commercial Drive. It was the last bastion of an old neighborhood that was being taken over by trendy gourmet shops and hemp clothing stores. At first sight, I wouldn't have said Roger was attractive. He had long blond curly locks in a ponytail, cascading down from a growing bald spot, as if he'd recently quit a heavy metal band but couldn't let go of the hair. He wore old jeans that bunched for yards around his calves and ankles, the extra material stopped from hitting ground by a huge pair of off-brand high tops, which he wore with their massive tongues sticking out. Underneath his plaid button-up, a promotional T-shirt of some sort, the logo indiscernible, poked out, making me think that most of his wardrobe came to him via T-shirt gun. But he did have a warm, inviting face and an authentic smile. He was thrilled to see me, and enthusiasm goes a long way. I joked with him about how

Gene was my pimp, and Roger responded with a high-pitched giggle that exposed a mouth of crooked teeth and made me wince.

Roger asked me about my life and seemed genuinely interested in my answers. I treated it like free therapy and opened up to him immediately. I didn't have to impress this guy, and it felt great to drone on about my dead-end job and shapeless life and how I was afraid to go to my apartment because of an evil gardener who yelled at me every time he saw the whites of my eyes. I left out the part where I fucked things up by fooling around with his friend. In commiseration, he told me how he was trying to get over his ex-girlfriend, but it was extra difficult because they had a baby together. He made it clear that the pregnancy was unplanned, that they had been acting foolishly, often "using her diaphragm as an ashtray." Now that was class. Although I was in no position to judge.

But when I asked what he did for a living and he responded, "I'm training to be a pastry chef," the wheel of fortune began to turn.

When Roger talked about his zeal for making pastries, he completely transformed, captivating me with his passionate and vivid descriptions. It was like poetic porn, the way he described gently folding fine layers of phyllo into perfect cones separated by chocolate drizzles and raspberry confit. I blushed as he mimed squeezing icing out of a pastry bag. Suddenly I saw someone passionate, accomplished, and admirable. He got so excited explaining this mango yellow pepper sauce that he grabbed my arm for emphasis and I felt tingles zip through my body. Now I wanted to see him work.

Our coffees turned into wines and day turned into night. His apartment was conveniently only blocks away. And we had sex. There was no hesitation on my part. His hands were like nothing I had ever experienced before. Maybe it was from working with delicate desserts or maybe he was born with it, but this guy had the most advanced sense of touch I'd ever come across. If it was learned, I wanted to call all his ex-girlfriends and thank them for their cumulative creation. I was helpless in his embrace. He knew when to caress lightly and when to add pressure, when to knead and when to baste, and when to add the right amount of sugar to make me want more. By the end, I needed a cooling rack. Plus, he was all about pleasing me, which in my twenties wasn't often the way with the boys. In the bedroom, Roger wasn't a messed-up 80s relic with a kid from a failed relationship; he was the romantic lead of every story. He wasn't just good in bed—it was his superpower.

Unlike me, who spent the majority of my life in my head analyzing, strategizing, and having fake arguments with dismissive store clerks, Roger had one sole purpose in life: to satisfy his senses. He asked what my favorite flower was, and I told him I loved that early summer smell of lilacs. The next night, he'd filled his bedroom with vases and vases of lilacs and replaced his nightstand light with a violet bulb. He was stunned that I had never listened to the opera *La Boheme* and played the CD loud enough so that we could take a steamy bath together while enjoying it. In the morning, he made me breakfast using cookie cutters to shape the hash browns into stars and hearts. It was the most sensual experience, and the sex got increasingly better. I was crème brûlée, and he was a flickering pastry torch.

After the baths, the flora, and treating me like a raspberry tart between the sheets, Roger talked about applying for pastry chef internships at impressive culinary schools around the country so he could really jumpstart his career. I wanted to be equally swept up about something in my world, so I talked about committing to this comedy thing, or at least getting good at it. I had a new "finger in a dyke" joke about my Dutch background that was starting to get laughs.

Roger and I dated for two months, but in a bubble. He did not clean up well, so there was no way in hell I was introducing him to anyone in my circle. We did not match or look good on or off paper, and it would be too hard to explain. I couldn't say, "Please, just let him go down on you and you'll get it!" And this was not one-sided. As far as I knew, he didn't have friends. Occasionally, I'd think I was being close-minded or shallow and should let someone in my life know about him, and then he'd arrive to meet me for lunch with a baby carriage in tow. I noted early on that I didn't particularly care for seeing him in daylight.

Our apartments were in the same neighborhood, making my secret commute very easy. Since he had three roommates and I had to be at work very early, I'd often leave his place at four in the morning so I could shower and blow-dry in my own home and still get to the train on time. One morning I was walking down the street toward the train station, passing in front of his apartment as I always did. I glanced at his door, and through the inlaid glass, I saw Roger standing there, smiling. He opened the door, handed me a freshly made café au lait and asked me to come in for a minute. He'd taken notice of my routine and had been waiting, knowing I'd walk by any minute.

He broke the news that he had been awarded a pastry internship at an exclusive hotel on Prince Edward Island and would be moving immediately. Again? Was I every man's last stop? Yet, I could only imagine how much better he would be after professional training—it would probably blow my mind. I was so happy for him. He'd be back in a year, he said, but we both knew this was it. We hugged and kissed and had sex right there in his kitchen at five fifteen in the morning. People say breakup sex is great, but nothing compares to *final sex*. You try to squeeze out every last drop.

While smoothing out my hair and using his phone to call Taxation Canada to say that I was running late due to food poisoning, Roger threw out the idea that I should take his room in the apartment. It would solve his immediate problem of finding someone, and it would set me free from the wrath of the livid landscaper. I agreed to meet with his roommates and talk it over.

At the beginning of the next month, I was living in Roger's room with the violet-colored bulb still in the nightstand lamp, and he was off to Prince Edward Island. My senses were starving. Now I missed two people that no one else in my life even knew about. A letter arrived from Roger, one scrawled page saying that he was so happy with his life, that the setting was breathtaking, and that he was learning how to shape strawberries into daffodils and make white chocolate lace. And that he missed his kid. And he missed me. I missed him too. Parts of him. I wouldn't say what we had was love, but it was strong and it was chemical. More like emulsion.

Roger and Gene were the best temp relationships I've ever had.

There was no upward mobility, no chance of a promotion, and no reason to settle in. We were mutual place-fillers for a real boyfriend or girlfriend, and it would have ended one way or another. I wish I could have created a Frankenmate, part Gene, part Roger, just add stylist! No one would ever believe at first sight that either of those two set the standard against which all future interactions in and out of the bedroom would be compared. I wondered who I was to them. Was I just an eager and willing participant wagging her tail whenever we hung out? A sounding board, a laugh track, a sous chef? I only hoped they thought I was funny.

CHAPTER 12

THE NICE FETISH

At twenty-six I hadn't accomplished much in my life, but I knew the difference between good and bad sex. People fail to mention that one of the side benefits of sleeping around is that you have a much better chance of stumbling across a gem or two. It's the law of slutty averages. And once you experience someone with real skills, it's very hard to go back.

I'd drawn a couple of conclusions along the way: Anyone who claims that they've had mind-blowing sex in the shower is lying. I'm not talking about erotic soaping up; I mean actual quality *sex* sex. Unless the water in your town has high KY levels, or you have the type of shower that includes a chaise lounge, it's impossible. Also, looks do not correspond with skill, and everyone has a fetish but me. I was even terrible at pillow talk. I couldn't figure out how to make it original or personal, but neither could anyone else. Dirty-talk standards seemed to be exceedingly low, and the questions were always the same, prompting responses that sounded like recycled porn copy: "Yes, it's so big. Yes, I'm yours. Yes, I like it. Yes, you're so hot." Ridiculous. It made me want to yell, "Quiet on the set! Stop asking and start working. If I like it, trust me, you'll know!"

I'd tried entry-level bondage, simply tying someone up to the four sides of the bed with some scarves. There was a certain amount of excitement to having him at my absolute mercy, until I wanted to free one of his hands but couldn't get the stupid knot undone. He started to panic, helplessly shackled to my bed frame, while I ran around the room naked, telling him to calm down as I tried to find scissors. Needless to say, I pushed the boundaries—in the wrong direction.

I had a theory that there were some things in life I shouldn't try, because if I liked them, the consequences would be too dire. It was the reason why I hadn't tried a strap-on dildo, shooting heroin, or disowning my family. Take the strap-on dildo for instance, arguably the tamest on the list: If I found out that having a plastic penis strapped to my abdomen unlocked a door to a room deep in my soul that had been secretly housing a miniature orchestra playing transcendent harmonies that moved me to tears of happiness, I would never again be able to settle for a simple C chord. Next I'd be seeking partners with similar interests, posting on Craigslist, and making room in my budget, let alone my closet. I wasn't ready for that level of dedication.

But if I'd ever been given an opportunity to explore with a boyfriend, it would have been with Mickey. Before I'd even set eyes on Mickey at a dinner party, the hostess made me promise that I wouldn't sleep with him. Could there be a more enticing buildup? She wasn't putting me on high alert because Mickey was a terrible person; she just didn't think our personalities would be a good match. I had no idea what she was talking about, plus I couldn't help myself; he was genetically blessed, classically good-looking in that hunky Italian way, but mixed with a bit of nerd. To this day, he is still the only man I've ever met who managed to make a calf tattoo of a flaming sun look sexy. And he liked me, I think. The hostess reported that after that dinner he referred to me as IMAX, because I was larger than life. I needed to find out what that meant.

Mickey stands out not only because he was so pleasant to look at but because he challenged me, in both good and not-so-good ways. I still love the things he introduced me to: the band The Magnetic Fields, the book *Geek Love*, and sea urchin sushi (uni). It didn't hurt that he had "play money"—a sizable family inheritance that he liked to spend in inspired ways. Out of the blue, he'd pick me up on a Sunday morning and announce that we were driving across the border to buy American beer and watch the Oscars on a motel room TV—just to, you know, "change things up."

During foreplay, Mickey would ask me what I wanted him to do, hoping that I'd suggest something wild. I never knew what to say. "Be nice to me? Hand wash my delicates? Explain the S&P 500 in a way that sinks in?" How do you say, "Just do the best version of what you're good at"? I could tell my responses let him down. I wasn't being very IMAX.

Always seeking adventure, Mickey suggested we take advantage of a last-minute deal and fly to San Francisco for the weekend. After we walked Fisherman's Wharf and enjoyed the audio tour of Alcatraz, he said that he'd like to check out the city's famous sex store Good Vibrations. I'd always thought that sex toys and vibrators were for people who weren't getting laid, but I didn't want to be a killjoy or a prude. He was so cool, I wanted to please him. And really—what was my big hang-up? I'd paid money to see Annie Sprinkle in college. I should loosen up. But it was one thing to see it, and another to do it.

I imagined a seedy store, full of middle-aged men in taupe raincoats stroking the plastic hair on the blow-up dolls. I couldn't have been more wrong. Good Vibrations was the friendliest shop I'd ever been to, period. We were greeted by a woman with a face full of piercings and a huge grin, who handed us a pink shopping basket and a condom. The whole place was showered in sparkles. There was literally an entire wall of shelves proudly displaying an array of pastel-colored, glitter-filled dildos. It was like Old Navy meets RuPaul's dressing room. Mickey held me close and told me to pick out anything I wanted. I wanted to hug him and say, "All I want is you, baby!" but felt I had to play along. I grabbed a white ostrich feather and placed it in the basket. All I needed was to find a bottle of self-heating massage oil and we were done. Mickey looked at the basket and through a brittle smile asked, "What else do you want?"

I swallowed and looked around. A bottle of water would be nice. It was like shopping for food on a full stomach. Nothing looked appetizing. With some help from another overly enthusiastic sales girl who showcased each toy as if it were second prize on a game show, we dropped $500. I was petrified.

Back in the hotel room, I packed all the new toys tightly into our suitcase; I didn't want the cleaning staff accidentally stumbling across them. Mickey had a different idea. He suggested we cancel our dinner reservations and check out our new products, like it was Kinkmas Eve. We started slow, with an ostrich feather. It was sweet and innocent, a little tickle here, a little giggle there, but I had no idea how few steps there were between an ostrich feather and a butt plug.

Mickey handed me a string of anal beads—which looked like a broken beaded bracelet—and told me to shove them up his ass one at a time and then slowly pull them out while he was coming.

What?!

I couldn't wrap my head around the basic logistics of this. What if I couldn't reach around? Would we need to drill holes in the bed or devise a pulley system? Wouldn't the timing need to be perfect? Could he throw a yellow flag to alert me?

We did it once, and then we did it again, and by the third time I sensed that this was going to be our new routine. Soon every sexual performance involved a prop. For the most part, I'll admit, I enjoyed it. I certainly understood what the fuss was all about. The toys did exactly what they were designed to do. They were fast, efficient, and reliable. But they weren't tender or sensual, nor did they unearth a secret philharmonic deep within my sexual soul. However, I did begin to associate an electric humming sound with an impending orgasm. I twitched in a room of fans.

The toys did not have the desired effect that I had in mind of strengthening the bond between us. It was hard to know whom to thank: the battery-powered machines and molded silicon or the handler. Whatever the case, I began to fantasize about good ole' basic sex. I don't care what anyone says; it's impossible to "make love" with anal beads up your ass.

As time went on, I also noticed that there was something mysterious about Mickey. Often, he was unable to sit still, uncomfortable in his own skin. He'd leave rooms to take phone calls, have vague obligations that he wouldn't discuss. I wouldn't hear from him for a few days and ask what was going on. He'd answer, "Oh, I had to help a friend move some furniture." I'd probe, "What friend? What furniture?" To which he'd answer, "Don't worry about it. You don't know them." I couldn't tell if he was cheating or was a spy.

How I felt about Mickey became synonymous with how I felt about Vancouver: There was something casually transient about all my encounters there—people seemed to drift in and out of one another's lives with no operatic drama, like smoke passing through a screen door. I was skimming the surface and could never dig in. We were all unmoored ships aimlessly floating around. There was nothing anchoring me down, other than my vague double A–battery relationship, and I started to think about moving again, this time to Toronto. This would continue my little dance of moving to a new city every time a relationship seemed doomed or fell apart. At least I was consistent at something.

Another day at the sewage-pump place ended, and I went over to Mickey's apartment, dropped my satchel, and sunk into his bean bag chair.

"I think I want to see what Toronto's like. Everyone says the stand-up scene is really good there."

"Oh yeah? I've always wanted to live in Toronto. This place is driving me crazy." Mickey's reply was unexpected. Was he suggesting we move there *together?* I felt as ambivalent about the idea as I did about our relationship.

"Well, do you think I should go out for a couple of months and see if it's any good?" I asked cautiously.

"Why not? You can store your stuff here for that month if you want. See what you think, and then I'll come out."

That made things almost too easy. I took his offer at face value and left a couple of boxes. Once again, I packed up my big blue backpack and headed east for an exploratory visit.

I'd only been in Toronto for two weeks, staying in a friend of a friend's apartment, when Mickey called to say he was coming to visit. He didn't *ask*, he *told* me, probably because he sensed that I was enjoying my new life without him too much and would protest if given the option. The second he arrived, it was clear that we were hanging on to each other by a fraying thread. He brought the sex toys with him, which I thought was a pretty ballsy move, considering he had to take them through airport security. I can only imagine what their outlines looked like on the TSA's monitors.

On his first night, I took him out for a nice dinner, hoping to lighten the mood, but he could barely conceal how pissed off he was at me for making him fly across the country to deal with the ambiguity of our relationship, and lashed out in bizarre ways. I'd lost five pounds due to stress, a rather insignificant amount, but Mickey commented that I was acting too proud of my "new body." I should have given him a gold star for noticing.

On the second night, he refused to leave my apartment. I couldn't understand why, and after we argued about how senseless he was being, I stormed out to do a spot on an open-mic comedy show. When I returned, I found him sitting in silence on the couch, holding my journal.

I froze. I knew what he'd read. It was my last entry from a few days earlier. I'd hung out with some improvisers after watching their show at Second City, and wrote about how one of them was particularly handsome. During the show, when he went into the audience asking for suggestions, calling out, "Can I get an object?" I yelled back, "How about my feelings?!" He thought that was hysterical, which inspired me to introduce myself after the show. The next thing I knew, we were kissing. And I described that. In detail. It was more than anyone should have to read.

Mickey was outraged that I'd broken his trust, and I was furious that he'd read my diary, but in the contest of who was the *most* wrong, we both lost. He called me an unfaithful bitch. I told him that he was a fucking lunatic. And thus began the most epic breakup of my decade, if measured in volume and destruction. We screamed and swore at each other. I called him a fucking asshole; he said I was a fucking bitch. It was unoriginal, fury-drenched dialogue, but I can tell you, we really sold it. This was the kind of dirty talk I could do.

He picked up the bottle of wine that we'd bought for dinner

and threw it. It smashed on the ground, glass shattering at my feet. I couldn't believe it. He looked at me, pleased with himself. I threw back the closest thing to me: the cheese it paired with. He tossed the camera he'd given to me as a going-away present while I madly ripped up photos of us and let the pieces fall in the air like confetti. There was a necklace, a T-shirt, and crumpled-up cards and love notes, all hurled through the air, but it wasn't until I felt a butt plug ricochet off my forehead that I knew it was O-V-E-R.

I threw the anal beads at his head and told him to stuff them up his own ass and pull them out one at a time while *leaving*.

He stomped out, but not without threatening, "You'll never hear from or see me again in your life."

Yeah, I assumed that after he read my diary and chucked a bottle at me.

The apartment was suddenly very still. I looked around at the wreckage littering my floor: torn photos, destroyed love notes, broken glass, plastic bits from the camera, and the sex toys. Without giving it too much thought, I grabbed a garbage bag and began furiously cleaning up, tossing it all in, until I got to the jewel vibrator "in tasteful silver."

Those sex toys were expensive and practically brand-new. I'd never be able to use them again or even look at them the same way. The butt plug was dead to me. Could I just boil them and give them away? Can you donate sex toys to Goodwill? Maybe I could run them through the dishwasher and give them to my neighbor? He was always loitering in the hallways wearing a smirk and a bathrobe. But then I'd have to talk to him. *Ew.*

I wanted to clear everything out of my life that had been even remotely connected to Mickey, literally and figuratively. So I sifted through my belongings and also tossed out *Geek Love*, all our remaining photos, and a bunch of CDs. I dragged the bag down to the back of the apartment building and hoisted it into the dumpster, savoring the image in my mind of the sanitation truck emptying that dumpster into a landfill, and amongst the rotting food, dirt, and debris, a big pink sparkly dildo proudly tumbling out.

I couldn't sleep that night. My mind raced through our fight, and my body wouldn't relax. I hated that we'd let things escalate to the point where we'd really never be able to talk again. I was pissed off at Mickey for ruining so many things. Going forward, not only would I never keep a journal again, but at bachelorette parties, if the bride whipped out a rabbit vibrator from a gift box, I would instinctively duck. I'd moved from fetish to phobia.

But at least I had someone to move on with.

A few weeks later I went to bed with the handsome improviser. It was a total relief that when he asked for a suggestion this time, he didn't ask for an object.

CHAPTER 13

RENT A WRECK

It was the dawn of a new millennium, and everyone was freaking out that after January 1 their computers wouldn't be able to keep time. I was living in a two-bedroom apartment above a secondhand bookstore in Little Italy, the coolest part of town. My roommate was a jazz musician dating a bassist, our upstairs neighbor was a makeup artist, and I was a struggling stand-up comedian in love with an improviser. We were all very impressed with ourselves.

Even though I lived there for four years, much of my Toronto Era was a blur. It was a particularly debaucherous time in my life, which is saying something. One of the city's many nicknames is Hogtown, as it used to be a livestock-processing center. I made sure I lived up to that moniker.

Sadly, the improviser and I weren't meant to be. We simply had different values. He wanted stability, companionship, and success in his career, and I wanted to PAR-TAY.

Now, even the word *party* makes me feel tired. I rebounded with anyone who showed a flicker of interest. He went on to date a taller, prettier, more successful version of me, a comedic actress named Olivia Rosenbaum. It was like he created her in his shed.

The epitome of the struggling artist, I worked ten different temporary jobs to make rent, and spent half the night at the comedy club hoping to get on, and the other half at the bar hoping to get off. Seeing as stage time was hard to come by, in the end, I'd built up a bigger reputation at my neighborhood bar than at Yuk Yuk's. This bar was called Ted's Wrecking Yard and had the atmosphere of an alcoholic's garage with a pool table in the back and a small stage for the occasional indie band. The combination of the pent-up energy from not getting on stage enough and the grungy atmosphere of Ted's transformed me into a different, more confident version of myself. My audience was the bartender and fellow patrons. The bartender even nicknamed me "the troublemaker," as I tried to impress him once by saying something ridiculous like "trouble relaxes me." Evidently, I watched too many episodes of *Knots Landing* as a kid. It was at this dark drinking establishment that I perfected the power of suggestion. I wasn't so much a tease as I was a taunt. Or a good improviser.

My method was as follows: I'd find a free bar stool and order a drink. If a guy sat down beside me, I'd say something like, "You can't sit here unless you buy me a drink, and I'm stealing one of your cigarettes." Then I'd order two Maker's Marks, turn back, and ask accusingly, "You do drink bourbon, don't you?" and lift my glass for a toast. Boldness goes a long way, and I had a pretty good return rate with this bulldozing technique. It was pre-foreplay role-playing. Most of the guys were caught off guard by my brash behavior and found it amusing. They'd usually pony up for a couple of drinks, engage in a little banter, and then sometimes we'd make out. I wouldn't leave with them, nor would we exchange info. It was a game I kept within the confines of the Wrecking Yard, which became my parlor, my acting workshop, my chemistry lab all rolled into one. It was shocking how easily these guys handed over the reins, completely content to sit back and see where I would take them. People love being told what to do.

One night I was even daring enough to approach this guy after watching his girlfriend storm out. Like a vulture, I swooped in with two shots of tequila, handed him one, and with a smile said, "Women. Can't live with them, can't stuff 'em in a bag." Like I said, I was a *struggling* comic. We clicked glasses, sucked on lemons, and followed up with a citrus-infused make out before last call. What I was doing was half harmless and half unhinged, but back then I had boundless energy for this sort of thing.

My fashion designer friend invited me to a party in New York, a trip I would remember for years because of how long it took to pay off that MasterCard bill. My flight left Friday morning at nine. The night before, I victoriously secured a date with Ethan from my new acting class. I developed a crush on Ethan even though the other actresses warned me, "He's the kind of guy who won't cushion your head as it's slamming into the headboard." That sounded less like a metaphor and more like something that had literally happened. Regardless, it was why I was attracted to him; I admired how he didn't seem to give a shit. He was who I pretended to be. And then there was the challenge aspect: What if I could make him protect my head?

We met for dinner at Ted's Wrecking Yard. Does Ted's serve food, you ask? No. Dinner was three rounds of beers.

"So are you seeing someone?" I asked him between rounds.

"Why? Do you have a suggestion?" he challenged.

"Yeah. How about the redhead over there?"

What did he think? I was an amateur?

"Already been with her," he volleyed back, and took another swig.

In a way, we were playing the same instant gratification game, both gatherers, not hunters. We weren't looking for one triumphant kill to drag home and feel proud of; we were content with racking up smaller scores.

Before we left, he insisted that "we needed" one round of shots, which would have made sense if they were vitamin B12 shots.

That's when I knew I'd broken through. Moments later, we kissed in my stairwell because I didn't want to disturb my roommate, who was studying for her jazz theory exam. Following a vigorous necking session that could only be classified as *hot*, he broke the action to look at his watch.

"Hey. I gotta go. I have tickets to this play," he said abruptly, putting on his leather jacket. He didn't invite me to join him. I acted unfazed.

"See you after New York," I said and waved, alluding that he might be missing his one chance, as the trip might change me. Some of those acting techniques we learned were proving useful.

I still had twelve hours until my flight—I could pack sixty-two times over! Since I was way ahead of schedule, I went back to Ted's Wrecking Yard in an effort to give the evening some resolve. This is what happens when you don't own a TV. The place was packed with mostly couples and people I already knew, so I ordered a draft and chatted with the bartender. A petite girl with translucent skin and short curly blonde hair wandered in and sat down beside me. She was dressed in a trashy tight polyester dress and heavily made up, but not enough to hide the dark-blue circles under her eyes. She looked like a tarted-up cherub on a bender. After drinking silently side by side for a while, I asked out of pure curiosity, "Are you waiting for someone?"

She snort-laughed. "No, I'm trying to get away from someone."

I liked that answer. "Well, let me know if I can be of help."

She introduced herself as Kerri, and we engaged in girl talk: sizing up and rating the different men in the bar. The alcohol started to hit me hard, and I remembered that I still had to pack. As I leaned down to grab my purse, I felt a small hand on my back. It was Kerri's. With bloodshot eyes she said, "I'll buy you a drink if you kiss me."

I wasn't opposed to the idea. My general philosophy was that it was hard enough to find someone you liked, let alone care what their gender was. I'd kissed a few girls along the way, but not much more, and never in public. The problem was, I didn't really want to. I've never been into blondes, and she was too short. I felt like a brute next to her. Then again, she did offer me an invitation to do something highly spontaneous and potentially entertaining. I gave Kerri the thumbs-up and grabbed her little head. I took special delight in the fact that the bartender saw me leave with Ethan a few hours earlier. As a matter of fact, his saliva was still fresh on my lips. I thought I was really pulling one over on life, playing a bigger game than everyone else. Of course, the bartender and other guys witnessing our display went nuts. They weren't frat boys as much as they were film students, so it was less hooting and hollering, and more encouraging catcalls, with a "Yay!" and a "Well done!" and a "Beautiful!" as if we were at an arty photoshoot. Drinks and shots piled up at the bar to encourage more action, the equivalent of putting quarters in the mechanical pony at the mall. The attention was far more exciting than the actual kissing; because of her size, I felt as if I were kissing a child or a miniature person. She had no real technique, and was clearly used to someone else doing all the work. Trashy blondes get away with everything.

Within the span of an hour, the making-out-and-pausing-to-do-shots show became a little repetitious, even for the spectators. Kerri asked if I wanted to go smoke a joint. It was absolutely the last thing I wanted to do, but my mouth was so unfamiliar with flexing the muscles needed to form the word *no,* that I agreed. I told her I lived a few steps away, and we could safely smoke it in the confines of my apartment. I couldn't decide if it was more or less dangerous to invite a strange woman versus a strange guy back to my place. Thanks to her size, I was pretty sure that if it came down to it, I could take her.

My roommate was practicing piano in the living room, so we snuck into my bedroom and smoked on my futon. As I was putting out the roach in the soil of my plant, Kerri began to disrobe. I exhaled. I didn't have the energy for this. But I couldn't ignore that I'd built up the expectation by inviting her up to my room. I'd mistakenly handed over the reins to her, happy to see where she would take me. Now she was offering another VIP ticket to a new experience if I wanted it.

I took off my shirt.

We rolled around on my mattress. She didn't know what she was doing, nor did I per se, so we fumbled around with zero finesse or expertise. Actual "getting off" was definitely out of the question, as it'd require dialogue, direction, sobriety, and time we didn't have.

A nauseous feeling started brewing in my stomach from the mixture of booze and general sensory overload, and I excused myself to the bathroom where I puked. I hung over the toilet for a moment, holding my hair with one hand, spit rolling off my lips onto the floor. My head was buzzing like it was full of cicadas, backed up by my roommate's frenetic jazz piano solo in the next room. Splashing water on my face and lapping it up from my cupped hands, I tried to talk myself back. *It's okay, it's okay. You're in a little over your head and turns out you can't handle everything. But it's okay, you just need to go to sleep. You're not going to die, you just need to sleep.*

I walked back into my bedroom to find Kerri waiting for me, draped seductively over my futon. I noticed that she'd refreshed her makeup, retouched her eyeliner, and added a bit of gloss. I found it was comical as I'd done the same thing many times before but had no idea how obvious it was. She smiled and ran her hands up and down her own body, which stirred my troubled stomach again. Her face turned to serious.

"You should know something," she said

Oh fuck. Was she about to tell me she had some sort of STD? I knew I should have at least grabbed some Saran Wrap from the kitchen.

She continued, "I'm married."

"Oh, thank god!" I said unintentionally out loud. I didn't care that she was cheating on her husband; as far as I was concerned I was cheating death. I had no desire to process what we'd done or bond over tea tomorrow morning. I needed to gargle with Listerine and get on a plane.

"I mean, it's okay. I'm with someone too. Listen, I have to go to New York in like four hours, so we should wrap this up for now and you should probably go home to your husband."

"What?" she said tersely. "You're kicking me out?"

I was definitely too tired for a brawl. I explained that I hadn't packed and the night got away from me. She angrily snatched her clothes off the floor and laced up her boots while muttering under her breath. It was the first time in my life I'd wanted to ask, *Why are you mad at me?* Whatever was going on in the minds of the guys at the bar was a thousand times better than what was actually happening here. I walked her to the door, and at the last minute she went in for a final kiss. I recoiled, mostly out of embarrassment that I smelled like vomit. She left in a huff, and I locked the deadbolt behind her.

Women.

I MISSED MY morning flight to JFK and resorted to paying extra to get a later one, a fee I accepted as a much-deserved irresponsibility tax. However, when I unzipped my bag in New York to get ready for the party, I discovered that I'd only packed one boot. With no time or money left to fix the problem, I wore a red cocktail dress with light-blue slip-on Vans to a fashion designer's party. I tried to laugh it off, admitting that this was the result of packing on the heels of a crazy night of corruption, but the New Yorkers were not impressed. It was one thing to fuck up your life; it was another thing to fuck up your footwear. At least I could run away quickly.

When I landed back in Toronto, exhausted and ashamed, I accepted that I'd reached my tipping point. Trouble wasn't relaxing me; it was ruining me. I promptly checked myself into a gym. As I ran on the treadmill facing a wall of mirrors, I wondered how long I could sit at Ted's Wrecking Yard before I became a broken-down pick-up truck that nobody wanted. And then I ran a little faster.

A few weeks later I was out for dinner with a friend, splurging on martinis. While I blathered on about my breakup with the impro-viser and recent wild escapades, I watched one of the waiters do a double take as he brushed by.

It took me a minute, but then I remembered him as the guy who waited on Mickey and me on our one good night in Toronto. He stuck in my memory because he had a serious Don Draper meets rockabilly look going on, with slicked-back hair and black-framed glasses. I had no explanation as to why he remembered me. Dear god, what had I done?

"Hey—how are you?" he asked warmly.

"I'm doing okay—surviving after a breakup!"

"I'm sorry to hear that," he said smiling.

A week later, that waiter showed up at one of my shows and sent a handwritten note backstage, asking me out. I was very flattered and accepted. The first thing I noticed on our date was that Henry wasn't a boy. He was a man, eight years older than me at that. The guys I'd manipulated at Ted's were like breadsticks taken out of the oven too soon. Henry was a fully formed, baked-to-perfection human with impeccable manners. He didn't claim to be a writer; he'd already been published numerous times. We dated for two and a half years.

Henry straightened me out and provided some much-needed stability, hypocritically the same sort of structure that I'd pooh-poohed while with the improviser. It was as if he installed a safety switch on me. I must have boosted his morale as well because during our time together both of our careers soared. I landed a half-hour comedy special for the Comedy Channel, and he quit his restaurant job to work full time as a movie critic and writer. I never had to pay to see a shitty movie again. He loved coming to my gigs, and if I bombed, he knew exactly what to say to reassure me that I was still on the right track. We talked until 4:00 AM every night, and I knew that kind of rapport was rare. My friends liked him—a lot more than they liked me—so we were regularly invited to dinner parties, events, and celebrations.

All in all, it was almost perfect. I've never gotten along with a boyfriend better than I did with Henry. Our relationship was cozy and intellectually stimulating, but as it progressed, a major problem surfaced: We didn't have a lot of sex. I thought of it as mind-body separation, or that we didn't match physically or chemically, but in my more vulnerable states I'd ask myself what was so wrong with me that he didn't want to jump me all the time? Or was this simply the way it was with long-term relationships? My mother claimed that she needed a team of eight men to cover her needs, as one to travel with, another to go dancing with . . . Could I have only one or the other—a guy to sleep with or a guy to be with? Henry and I made model partners and roommates, but I feared that sooner or later, in frustration, he'd hire a hooker and I'd blow our neighbor.

Toronto started to pale, like a favorite dress that didn't fit anymore. Anytime I asked people if they'd ever thought about leaving, they'd respond with an emphatic "No! Are you kidding? Why would you leave this place? It's got everything New York has minus the grit, crowds, and crime." I hated the Toronto/New York comparison. It illuminated how much of a self-esteem issue Toronto had. If I argued and said something like, "Well, it doesn't have Broadway or the Empire State Building," they'd shoot back, "Actually, Toronto has the third largest English-speaking theater scene in the world, and don't tell me you've never been to the CN Tower?!" It reminded me of being a kid and griping to my mother, "Tracy's mom let us eat cookies for dinner," to which she would respond, "Well then, why don't you go live at Tracy's?" Now that I was all grown up, I wanted to see if I could hack it at Tracy's.

When I mentioned moving to New York to my sister, she recommended that I do it quickly because the older you get, the less you can put up with ANYTHING, let alone moving to a foreign country and living like a college student. She implied there was only a sliver of time between finding a sublet in Brooklyn and settling into assisted living in Boynton Beach.

Of all the things I had done, this seemed the riskiest. What if I failed? What if someone drugged my drink and tried to steal my lung? At least my scar would confuse them. They'd think someone else on their team had already gotten to me.

One autumn evening, Henry came over for dinner. I loved my kitchen in that apartment. It contained the most expensive furniture I owned, a Formica table with chrome legs and matching pink chairs. There was no overhead light, just three shaded lamps, so it always felt moody. My roommate set up her portable CD player on top of the fridge, and we listened to the song I was addicted to at the time, Wyclef Jean's "Gone till November." The song's probably about drugs, but I interpreted it as being about traveling for your career.

The night took an unexpected turn when Henry started the conversation with, "I've been thinking . . . "

I don't know if he could smell my inner turmoil, but he had been mulling over the idea that perhaps it was time for us to take the next step and get a place together. This was no small decision for him. I'd pushed the issue occasionally, but he always seemed adamant that the timing wasn't right. Eventually, I'd concluded that either he'd gone through one too many failed relationships and was now stuck in his ways, or he didn't like me enough. Something must have changed his mind, but I'll never know what, because instead of a tearful "Yes! I would love that!" what fell out of my mouth instead was "I'm moving to New York."

We both couldn't believe what I said. He stared at his plate. I held my breath. Wyclef Jean sang, "See you must understand, I can't work a nine to five, so I'll be gone till November, said I'll be gone till November . . . "

"Well," he said after a while, "if that's what you need to do, I'll help you do it."

That sounded compassionate and sweet, but for the record it's different from "I'll move with you," or "What the hell are you talking about?" or "Fuck you, we're breaking up."

Who says that? *I'll help you leave?!* After that, why don't we go on Match.com together? Was I being conveniently dismissed?

There's being supportive and then there's being overly supportive, which creates the opposite effect.

But I needed a lot of help, so foolishly I accepted his.

Here's another rule: Never let anyone you've slept with in the past year help you move away. Somehow, while you're slapping a tape gun across a cardboard box, you'll pack up all the nice feelings you had for each other in those containers. Break up with them fast and dirty, and then put all your prized possessions on the street with a sign that reads FREE STUFF. Trust me, you won't remember what's in half those boxes a year down the line.

It was my last night in town—in theory. That is, if I didn't come back the next month with my tail between my legs. I'd already given away my room and my Formica table to another girl who squealed in delight when she noticed how close the apartment was to Ted's Wrecking Yard. It was as if I passed her the hussy baton. I stayed at Henry's that night, and the mood was bittersweet. After all, I was moving to New York without a job or a fragment of an opportunity waiting for me, abandoning four years of my life and one long-term relationship. I was both terrified and guilty, which meant I couldn't wait to leave.

I'd booked an insanely early bus out. Henry said I looked tired.

"Well then, let me sleep tonight, okay? Don't try anything," I said with a wink. He assured me nothing would happen. I gave him that "Really?" look and tried to fall asleep, but I couldn't. I couldn't believe nothing was happening! No accidental brush high on my thigh, no goodnight kiss that lingered, no poking in the small of my back. Nothing.

CHAPTER 14

SCREW NO ONE

In late July of 2001, I stuffed my life savings of $600 into my wallet, strapped on my blue backpack teeming with high heels and hope, and boarded a bus to Toronto's Pearson Airport. I'd purchased a round-trip ticket to New York, with the intention of never using the flight back. Henry came with me to the bus station, mostly to make sure that I was actually leaving. As the bus peeled out of the parking lot, I waved to him from my mud-stained window. He smiled and waved back. We kept with the upbeat grinning and waving until the bus turned onto the street. He must have thought he was out of view, but I caught one final glimpse as we turned the corner and saw him break down into a fit of tears. I'd seen him cry a little during a sad movie, but I'd never witnessed anything like this. It was heavy, painful sobbing. His face contorted and his mouth hung open in agony. I felt trapped inside of that moving bus, passively watching the drama, like a reality television cameraman. I had no idea he'd react like that. Maybe if I had, I wouldn't have packed up so quickly. In a twisted way, he was so pro–me moving to New York that I thought if I backed out, I'd disappoint him. Then again, the fact that I wanted to skip town in the first place probably sent a clear message that I didn't see us going anywhere, or why else would I leave? Couples therapy could have straightened this whole mess out, and instead of me leaving and him crying, we'd be having brunch.

The inadequacy of my entire plan suddenly dawned on me. Was I really moving to New York with no comedy connections and no status, starting from scratch, with only enough money to last me a couple of months? Who did that clichéd move-to-The-Big-Apple-bags-in-hand thing anymore? I didn't even know how to tap dance! Was I running away, or was I honing in on what I wanted? The anxiety from the barrage of all these unanswered questions caused a panel in my brain to overheat, and I sank into a meditative state numbly watching the moving landscape. If everything went as planned, I would have years to second-guess myself. One thing I did have was a friend who offered to put me up in her apartment for "as long as it takes," which elevated her to the "yes, I will help you move a dead body" category of friendship.

I found out that "as long as it takes" translated to "until my boyfriend moves in," a measure of time that equaled two months (lowering her down a notch into the "yes, I will travel for your wedding" category of friendship). Still, it was an incredibly generous gesture from someone who lived in a tiny, windowless basement covered in a blanket of cat hair with a hot plate for a stove.

Not only was I one of a million so-called stand-up comics who were trying to "make it," but it took a while for my Canadian accent to fade, and I unintentionally gained most of my laughs from saying words like "garburator," "chesterfield," and "washroom." "Aboot" was my big closer. It wasn't funny; it was cute.

I glommed on to a group of my girlfriend's girlfriends, whom I referred to as the "clickity-clack gals" on account of how their heels sounded on the pavement. These women were effortlessly stylish. They knew how to accessorize and seemed to come from impressive pedigrees. They weren't my soul mates, but I was happy to hang around them, even if we had nothing in common besides our gender. I felt bucktoothed and small town in their company. Even my shoes looked square and clunky next to theirs. But listening to them talk about how they dealt with guys was an exercise in restraint. I wanted to shake each of them and scream, "Just fucking call him already, for god's sake!"

Why were these beautiful, successful, smart women squandering their time analyzing why some art director didn't call them back? Was there something in those blood-orange margaritas that made them question their worth? It took me a long time to understand that I'd been playing the demo version of the dating game for all those years. This was the advanced edition. *Sex and the City* wasn't a parody. It was a documentary.

The clickity-clack gals warned me that New York men were demanding and fickle. For example, they said, no man within the five boroughs would sleep with me unless I got a Brazilian wax. Really? Even Staten Islanders? I'd never heard of guys with grooming preferences. As a matter of fact, I was under the impression that not only would they take what they could get, but they wouldn't so much as blink an eye if you were *covered* in fur, as long as it didn't get in the way of them sticking it in. Were the rules so vastly different three hundred miles south of the border? But the girls stuck by their assessments, so I made an appointment with the Korean waxer who worked in the back of a salon called E-Nail. When she saw what she'd be dealing with she yelped, "You're like monkey-girl!" loud enough to echo throughout the rest of the salon. Did I seriously have to tip this woman?

I learned an interesting fact: I had a very small window of time to make the best of that expensive bikini wax. Being half Israeli, it was about forty minutes.

The clickity-clack gals invited me out to a trendy SoHo bar with a gaggle of guys with whom they had ambiguous relationships. As last call approached, everyone circled around one another like some sort of intoxicated square dance, trying to find a final partner. Worried that it was going to be junior high dodgeball all over again, I excused myself to stand by the bar, hoping to avoid the shame of being picked last. While holding a twenty-dollar bill in my hand, jammed in a sea of cute people, it struck me that being self-conscious about my scar was the least of my problems; I wasn't sure I even had the genetic gifts to get the attention of the bartender.

One of the guys from the group wound up standing beside me. He sported a surfer-boy style with messy hair and a braided rope bracelet that seemed totally out of place in Gotham's gloominess.

Without any direction from me, he caught the bartender's eye and ordered us both double vodkas on the rocks. Either he was trying to get me into bed or he had a drinking problem. Either way, I was in. With my eye on my Blue Crush prize, I laughed too hard at everything he said and subtly let it slip out that my apartment was only a few blocks away and I had a six-pack chilling in the fridge. Oh, and my roommate was out of town.

"We should go there right after we have one more, right?" he suggested. I stood corrected: It wasn't *or* he had a drinking problem— it was *and* he had a drinking problem.

"Nothing fruity," I requested.

I felt so superior leaving with his arm around my neck in front of my new friends who'd warned me that the men in this city were impossible. Really? Because it appeared that I'd mastered the situation in a matter of weeks. This place was just like Toronto.

Back at my apartment, I was all aflutter, contemplating how to create the perfect surfer's paradise. I handed him his as-advertised-in-the-brochure bottle of Heineken and finally settled on a stunt I'd never tried before. Without warning, while sitting on the couch, I unzipped his jeans and pushed my own head down. It was the perfect mixture of spontaneity, confidence, and filth. I reemerged after a few minutes to receive my "job well done" gratitude and reciprocation. He grazed the side of my cheek with the back of his hand and said, "You're amazing. Thank you for the freebie." I giggled along at his little joke and waited for him to walk me to the bedroom. Instead, he used the momentum to grin his way right out my front door.

As the door shut behind him, I stood there frozen, feeling the smile fade from my face. Did I get taken advantage of? Did that poor man's Kelly Slater drink my beer, take my blow job, and say aloha without even asking for my number? Not only was it bad manners, but who walks away from a simple one-night stand? Was I so undesirable that he didn't even want to entertain having casual sex with me? I cracked the remaining Heineken and paced around my apartment like a detective working on The Case of the Missing Orgasm. Maybe this was a misunderstanding and I should forget about it. Or maybe my drunken blow job was a little toothy? In hindsight, I hoped so. Still, I felt silly about my whorish display.

I should have never doubted the clickity-clack gals. Like prehistoric fish crawling out of the ocean, they'd adapted and evolved to deal with the cruel world they were presented with. There had to be another way. When I relayed the perturbing tale to one of them the next day, she was totally unphased. "Yeah, I think something similar happened with Elicia and that guy."

Wait, so this guy had struck before but no one warned me? Or marked him with a red *X*? Was this part of my initiation? No. I refused. I would not join their ranks. Like the famous girl-surfer whose arm was bitten off by a shark, I too had to dive back in.

ONE OF THE advantages of being a female stand-up comic was that I ran in a circle of mostly single men—damaged, childish, social weirdos, but still identifiable as men. A few months after my blown blow job experience, I met a comic who I thought was an exception to the introvert/freak rule. Niche shows were the new hook, and after performing on *Chicks and Giggles* and *Yids in the Hood*, I landed a spot on a dating-themed show called *Singularly Hilarious*. Since the major requirement of the show was that you were unattached, the green room was like a cramped, awkward, singles mixer. This comic was by far the cutest in the room, although that wasn't saying much. He dressed a little too preppy for my taste, as if he'd rushed there from his day job on Wall Street, and he wasn't particularly warm or expressive. In the place of a smile, he raised the right corner of his mouth. At least he'd never get wrinkles. His idea of flirting was asking me, "Why haven't I met you yet?" which could have easily translated to, "Did I already have sex with you and you've changed your hair, or are you a different girl?" I replied, "I guess because I have a better booking agent." He took the insult with a lopsided smirk and asked if I would like to go on a date some time. An actual date. I was impressed.

We met at a loud and crowded bar, where we drank whiskey, and then I dragged him down a hallway and through a door marked STAFF ONLY to frenetically make out. He didn't ask questions along the way, just followed. It was like old times. After getting kicked out by a screaming busboy, we staggered down the streets and he flashed me a look that said, "You're not like the other girls, are you?" I totally basked in it. That's right, I was different. We walked in the direction of his apartment, a loft that he shared with a graffiti artist. I was about to say, "Isn't that the same as saying you live with a criminal?" but he asked a better question first.

"Have you ever spray-painted public property before?"

"Of course not!" I laughed. I liked this guy. He was seeing my bet and raising me.

"It's a great way to let off some steam, you know?"

No. But I was about to.

A metal bookshelf of partially used spray-paint cans in a rainbow of colors stood in the front entrance of his apartment. He grabbed a black can, I requested orange, and we headed down the block to a building under construction. Its facade was covered with temporary raw plywood walls that were already tagged, postered, and splattered. He sprayed a zigzag across the wall to show me how it was done, and I added a simple neon orange circle above it. Vandalizing public property was incredible. Not only because of the rush associated with the thought of being caught, but because it was so liberating to mark New York like I owned it. It didn't control me; I controlled it. Take that! Soon we were running up and down the block, giggling and coating the walls with black and orange shapes. I was overtaken by the moment and thought, *This is how real relationships start. This is the story we'll tell people.* Or, as it turned out, I'd tell people.

He drew a sad face with heavy black dots for eyes that ran down the wall like mascara tears and signed his initials. I wrote "self-portrait" underneath it. He gave me the lip raise that suggested we head back to his apartment before someone saw us.

Back at his apartment, he introduced me to his loft bed, a space-saving structure specific to small city apartments, basically an upper bunk-bed. Everything in this city was exhausting; even foreplay involved climbing a ladder. Half-clothed, lying down with our heads four inches from the ceiling, we fooled around until he plainly asked, "Should we have sex?"

"I want to, but I can't," I answered definitively.

"C'mon. Why not?"

I couldn't say, *Because the dude before you ruined it for everyone, okay?*

"I can't right now." I didn't care that it probably sounded like I had my period, or that I was between waxes, or that the rash was back.

"But we're right here."

I'd used that argument before.

"I'd love to, but it's a no." I sounded like a judge on *Star Search*.

He lazily tried to convince me for a few more minutes, but I stuck to my guns and finally we fell asleep. The next morning, on my way out, he asked if I'd like to meet up later in the week for a drink, so I figured I'd made the right choice. Write it down. Don't ever give it up on the first date.

I spent way too much time getting ready for that next drink. Usually I allotted about forty-five minutes, but this time I gave myself a full ninety to thoroughly shave, pluck, prime, and paint. While adding the finishing touches of long dangly earrings and spraying jasmine-scented perfume on every crease of my body, I thought, *Tonight I will have sex with this man. He deserves it.* My outfit worked every angle: a low-cut blouse and a short skirt, thigh-high stockings with high heels, big red lips, and smoky eyes. Before I clickity-clacked out the door, I threw a toothbrush and a pair of fresh underwear into my purse, like a pro.

I'd chosen this candlelit lounge that always had some atmospheric Portishead-inspired mix playing in the background. He seemed different from the last time: distant and even harder to read. I couldn't penetrate his dour mood or make that corner of his lip rise. The connection we'd had the first night, however shallow, was gone. I couldn't hit upon how things had gone awry. He gave me no choice but to begrudgingly ask, "So, is something wrong?"

"I'm going through a bout of depression. I'll probably go home after this beer."

One beer? My vision for our evening was slipping from my grips. In an attempt to buy some time to turn things around, I posed that we split one more beer and then I'd release him into the night. He went for it, slammed down his half, and announced he was leaving.

"Can I come with you? I promise to make you feel better. I can be like a huge dose of Prozac!" My last resort was to compare myself to pharmaceuticals.

"No, I really need to go home . . . alone."

Once again, I was completely baffled.

It started to rain, and we stood outside under my umbrella saying good-bye.

"I guess have a good night!" I said sarcastically.

"I'm sorry, Ophira," he said. He tried to kiss me, but I moved away.

"No trial prescriptions," I snapped. It was a dumb comeback, but it was all I could come up with while feeling rejected.

He sort of shrugged as if it were worth a shot and walked away. I knew I couldn't both run after him and keep my integrity. With a sigh, I pivoted on my heels and headed back home, sloshing through the puddles and soaking my feet because I couldn't take large strides in my constrictive skirt.

When I returned to my apartment, I stared at myself in the mirror, dumbfounded. A frosted-up face of heavy makeup with huge gold dangly earrings returned my glare. I looked like a fucking clown. Or a gypsy. Or a gypsy clown, the most hated variety of clown. What was he even apologizing for? For voting me out of his life?

There seemed to be no correlation between cause and effect. Give it up on the first date, don't give it up on the first date, neither worked. The magic formula was beyond me. Again I questioned, who was too depressed to have sex? These New York guys were so . . . sensitive.

I tried as hard as I could to resist wallowing in the "what's wrong with me?" debate and instead concentrated on how much of a jerk that guy was, but still it got to me. I didn't need any eye makeup remover that night, as I cried most of it off in big black drops of tar: his graffiti portrait brought to life. Oscar Wilde was right again—life does imitate art.

I e-mailed him a few days later, some lighthearted, carefully worded e-mail about picking up where we left off whenever he was "around." No big deal! He didn't reply. Shortly after, I was out with some female comic-friends, and after a few Merlots I spilled the whole story. One of the women tried to comfort me by saying, "I dated that guy like five years ago, and you know what I think? I think he doesn't like women." No shit. I was starting to hate men, so I understood. How could these guys have waxing preferences on one hand and not even like women on the other? What was the point of figuring out this stupid town? Was it even worth it? I couldn't believe I was getting dumped before they knew me well enough to accuse me of being needy, self-involved, dramatic, or unfaithful. These hasty rejections triggered the big insecurities, like *I wasn't good enough. Maybe I didn't compare in the bigger pond. Maybe I should get a nose job.* As a comic with a telemarketing job, I couldn't console myself by thinking, *Well, at least I have my fabulous career! Time for a little retail therapy—watch out Theory sample rack!* I imagined that all other New York girls could cry on the phone to their parents, who'd immediately book them for a rejuvenating facial to dry those tears in expensive clay, but I didn't have that privilege. I could console myself by heating up a can of Chunky soup and clicking through the channels, hoping to come across a sitcom like *Friends* or *Frasier*, where everyone always wins.

Confiding in the clickity-clack girls did nothing to alleviate my aggravation. They were just as unhappy, continuously griping that they couldn't find "the one." I didn't give a shit about "the one." I was still working on "anyone." God, this was nothing like Toronto.

I told them that I didn't want to find a husband, that I didn't even believe in marriage, and that my grandmother, on her deathbed, said to me, "Never get married or have kids. They will ruin your life." My mother was no different, warning me that once you wed, your identity would be whittled down to housewife, nursemaid, or babysitter. Is that what they wanted? Plus, who moves to New York City to settle down? That's why you leave!

I didn't hear much from the clickity-clack gals after that rant.

I would absolutely not bitterly swear off men, nor would I google "silent meditation retreats." What I would do was go in the other direction. These guys needed to know that they shouldn't flatter themselves by thinking I wanted a commitment from them. I didn't even want their one pillow. I was here to do stand-up. But it'd be nice to share a bottle of wine with someone and get naked occasionally. How about we don't get to know each other? How great would that be? Why doesn't anyone ever talk about the merits of never meeting his family?

My mantra echoed the sentiments in the poem on the plaque at the Statue of Liberty ("Give me your tired, your poor . . . "). I wouldn't discriminate. I could make up for not having supermodel-like looks by focusing once again on my best quality: I was not picky. Or as I liked to see it, I was open. A bunk bed is still a bed.

I needed to summon that same character I'd created for myself at Ted's Wrecking Yard, just mature it and toughen it up a bit. I consciously shelved the softer side of my personality and became a slightly brasher, more removed, less caring version of myself. I saw it like putting on a bulletproof vest. It wasn't that I was playing hard to get; on the contrary, I was very easy to get. But vulnerability had no place here. I'd give it up when I felt like it, go home early when I felt like it, hit on his friend if I felt like it. This was all about me.

Shortly after making this mental decision, I was asked out by a handsome Middle Eastern man with biceps of steel. We'd met performing in a show on Long Island. He was a newer stand-up comic, and terrible at it. I mean absolutely terrible. I didn't know what he was doing on stage other than throwing around some ego, but unlike the other girls, I couldn't care less if a guy made me laugh. He fulfilled my basic criteria: He asked me out.

The second we sat down he grabbed my hands. "Do you know how beautiful you are?" As cheesy as it was, it still made me look away. How do you respond to that? "Yes, I do. Thank you for acknowledging it. Now let's proceed with our date." Any over-the-top compliment like that smells of bullshit. How often did he throw that particular move around? A good-looking guy like him probably dated a dozen models, flight attendants, and commercial actresses. A voice in my head interrupted my train of skepticism and berated, *Can't you shut up and enjoy yourself?* We ordered a couple of pints, and his cell phone rang. He sprang up to answer it and turned toward the outside patio, waving his arms at an approaching SUV while yelling, "I'm right here! Do you see me?"

"I'll be right back, gorgeous!" he said, while vaulting over the short patio fence and running toward the SUV. Maybe he forgot something at a buddy's and they were coming back to give it to him? Or it was a surprise flower delivery for the girl who doesn't know how beautiful she is? That's all I could come up with to explain the situation. When he returned empty-handed, I tried my best to feign nonchalance.

"What was that all about?"

"I had to get something from a friend."

I involuntarily raised an eyebrow but heard that inner scolding voice again. *Let it go. It's a first date. Who cares, remember?*

After the eighth time he excused himself to go to the bathroom, I started to get a clue as to what he got from his "friend."

"Hey, are you doing coke in the bathroom?" I asked.

"Yeah. Why? Do you want some?"

It was seven on a Monday night.

"No, I'm fine, thanks. I'm more of a Thursday through Saturday kind of girl."

"It's not like I have a problem, gorgeous. It's just for a little fun."

I didn't want to show my displeasure or chastise him by pointing out that nothing says "a problem" like blatantly scoring drugs on a first date, but I was done. I could overlook a lot of things, but a narcissist cokehead took too much effort. We were probably two lines away from him telling me about some million-dollar business idea he had, followed by tears remembering the day his family had to put down his childhood pet. I finished my beer, placed the empty glass on the counter, and laughed to myself out of utter exasperation.

"I gotta go," I said, dispirited.

He guzzled the rest of his beer. "I'll walk you to the subway."

Even though I lived within walking distance, I didn't refuse him. I could tell he knew he'd fucked up, and he was not a complete jerk. We walked a block in silence. All of a sudden he became agitated, grabbed me by the waist, and started kissing me in the middle of the street. My first impulse was to push him away, but one of my one thousand weaknesses was a good make out. I don't know whether it was the actual skill or whether it was the coke, but he was an excellent kisser. It completely clouded my better judgment.

Having a good time now? my inner asshole voice mocked.

"Let's go to your place," I said.

"How about your place?" he whispered with his eyes closed, still kissing me like Pepé Le Pew.

"No good," I said, trying to catch my breath. "My roommate's in town and it's a one bedroom. Weird situation. It wouldn't work."

"Yeah? Well, my girlfriend's at mine . . . "

This time I pried him off me. It was one thing after another with this dude. It was impressive.

"We're almost broken up, seriously. How can you blame me? Who could resist someone like you?" he said, as charming as possible.

I asked him to explain the situation, and the real story flooded out of him. He was married, maybe separated, maybe they'd had a bad argument, living in the suburbs of Long Island. Apparently, he was happy to take the train into Manhattan on a Monday to do some blow and try to get blown by some dumb Canadian girl who would fall for the "doesn't know how beautiful she is" line.

"Actually, I need to go, but we'll get it figured out next time," I said, firm but gracious. No need to throw the train off its rails.

"One more kiss before you go then?"

I agreed. What the hell? And we made out on the sidewalk for a few more minutes.

"I'll call you!" he said, as we went our separate ways. Yeah. That's the guy who's going to call me.

I walked home through the West Village, disheveled and dizzy on a mixture of beer and pheromones, wondering if this was how it was going to go from now on. It wasn't a total loss of a night. It was kind of great: free beer, crazy guy, awesome make out. And now I was done, and it was only 8:30 PM. I still had the whole night ahead of me.

AFTER SIX MONTHS in New York, I flew home to see my family in Calgary for a much-needed break. It was the holidays, and I relished in the luxuries of a normal-sized fridge full of food, a washer/dryer on the premises, and nothing to do. My mother was in the basement going through her pickling and I was chopping tomatoes for a salad, when the phone rang. Before I picked it up, I glanced at the caller ID out of habit, and was surprised to recognize the number. There are a few phone numbers that stick in your mind forever.

It was Michael.

We'd had some contact over the years, mostly through e-mail, and still shared a few friends. I'd heard that he was engaged.

It took me three rings to pick it up. *Why the hell was he calling?*

"Hello?"

"Hey, Ophira! It's Michael!"

My birthday was in a few days, and Michael had remembered. He assumed that I'd probably be in Calgary visiting my mother. He was right. I asked him how he was, how his mom was . . . he returned the same questions and conversational pleasantries and wished me a happy birthday.

"So it's the big 3-0, huh?" he said.

"Yeah, I'm getting old!"

"Remember when you were, like, twenty you said that if we both weren't married by the time you were thirty that we should give it another shot?"

"Yes." I chuckled, embarrassed by that desperate, heartbroken girl I was in the past. "Oh god. I'm sorry about that. Jesus. And I heard you're engaged, right? Congrats on that! When do I meet her?"

The line went silent for a minute.

"Oh, *ah*, no, that didn't end up happening. I'll tell you about it another time. No, as things stand right now, you're about to be thirty, and we're both not married."

I took my turn at being quiet.

"What do you think?" Michael asked.

"What do you mean?" Even though I knew.

"Do you want to give us another shot?"

I couldn't believe this was happening. The former love of my life, whom I couldn't get over for years and years, now wanted a second shot. Now.

Did that Come Back to Me spell finally take? *Now?*

No one had compared to him, but everything had changed since. With full confidence, my answer rose up from deep within my soul. It was so clear to me.

"No."

What can I say—a lot had happened in ten years. I wasn't that young, misguided girl anymore who looked up to him like he was some sort of deity. I'd been forced to move on, and then on again. And I was certainly not willing to be his Plan B.

I don't think Michael envisioned our call going that way.

"Really? Are you seeing someone?"

"No, well . . . not really. I mean, yes, I am. It's hard to explain. Anyhow, I would love to see you for a drink while I'm here," I chirped, switching gears.

We arranged to meet for a drink, which was very nice, with a lot of stilted conversation, but I don't think either of us ever want to do that again. At least we were even.

I'd like to say that I felt something reignite inside of me or was devastated over the timing. But the truth was, it was one of the best days of my entire life. That voodoo witch doctor was better than I thought. Although she may have ignored my request and gave me the Move On with Your Life spell instead. I would never know. But I was ready to return to New York.

CHAPTER 15

GOODNIGHT, CHARLIE

Comedy was starting to pay off. I'd worked really hard at my material and landed my first American TV spot on a Comedy Central show called *Premium Blend*. Following that, I booked a slew of road work that included featuring at a high-caliber comedy club in Raleigh, North Carolina. I thought, *Wow. It's happening. I'm starting to make it as a stand-up.*

My only obstacle was loneliness. I hated road loneliness—it was like being the unpopular one in a threesome. I vowed that Raleigh would be different: I'd be productive in my downtime, work on my act, read books, write TV pitches, maybe even explore the city. When I packed for that week, I didn't just overpack: I overoptimistically packed, as if I was going to become a better version of myself while there. I brought a fresh notebook, a manual on how to become an amateur CSI (in case I needed a job to fall back on), a jump rope, and an exfoliating mud mask.

The second I set my bag down in that dark hotel room, my hopefulness evaporated and I started to panic. Five minutes later, depression had completely overtaken me. I called a couple of friends, but my calls went straight to voice mail. The only other ongoing relationship I had was with coke-addict guy. I had to hand it to him, he said he'd call, and he did—relentlessly, for almost a year. In an effort to stop myself from scrolling through my contact list and assessing each name in terms of the quality of our friendship, I flipped on the TV and clicked through all the channels, twice. Then I rummaged through the room and found the Bible, the Koran, a few takeout menus, and a postcard advertising female escorts on the front, male on the back. This hotel catered to an eclectic crowd.

I arrived at the club on the desperate side of early. It was a Tuesday, but the headliner didn't arrive until Thursday, so for the next two nights I was the main attraction. When I hit the stage two hours later, I was transformed into everyone's best friend for the next forty-five minutes. It was such a relief, and I left the stage sporting a nice comforting buzz. As far as I was concerned, my only post-show obligation was to keep the high going, so I headed straight to the bar and threw twenty bucks on the counter. The bartender informed me that headliners drink for free. *God, I love being a headliner,* I thought, while ordering a Grey Goose on the rocks. I told him to keep the twenty as a tip. Then I showed my self-control to the door.

Several Gooses later, I found myself scanning faces at the bar, all of them men, looking for someone to flirt with, someone to play with. This wasn't about choice. It was about survival. Then I spotted my target: a tall, lanky bar back who seemed like the silent type. I grabbed my beer, wandered over to him, and said, "Are you like the dark horse of this place or something?" That was my opening line. It sounded so much better in my head on the walk over. It's harder being a guy than it looks.

He smiled back, which disrupted the whole dark horse thing as it revealed that he was really young. Like early twenties. If I squinted, midtwenties. He was no dark horse. He was a dark pony. But he was my dark little pony.

We proceeded to drink and drink. Dark Pony mentioned that he was still in college, but I didn't want to know what year. I didn't actually want to talk about anything; I just liked the mixture of flirtation and alcohol. It was well after last call, and they wanted to close up the club, but I didn't want the evening to end. I would do anything to not go back to that miserable abyss of a hotel room. As if he heard my drunken battle cry, Dark Pony asked, "Do you wanna come over to my place and smoke some pot?" Oh god, yes.

While he gathered the rest of the empties, I sobered up for a second. Was it a terrible idea to go off with some strange young-adult bar back to an undisclosed location in an unfamiliar town to smoke pot? I looked at my phone like it was an oracle, but all I saw was that there were no new messages and no missed calls.

Dark Pony returned with a faded jean jacket on.

"Let's go," I said.

His place was a classic college boy's apartment—stark and beige. There wasn't one piece of art on the walls. I opened the fridge to look for a Brita only to find a pizza box containing no pizza and a bottle of ketchup so ancient it had stratified into dark-red and brown layers. We sat on his beige futon and shared a joint. Usually I can keep my composure through just about anything, but his pot was like nothing I'd ever smoked before, and I felt beyond fucked-up after two quick hits. My hands turned to ice. Paranoia overtook me, and I was suddenly very self-conscious. I began to question everything: *Did Dark Pony see my set tonight? Did he think it was funny? He didn't mention anything. Did he find me attractive? Or did he think I was too old for him? Why are women still not respected enough in comedy? I need Joan Rivers to talk me down. Why don't I have more female role models? Should I wait another night before I try anything with him?*

A male voice interrupted my runaway train of thought to ask, "Do you wanna do a gravity bong?"

"Yeah, okay."

A gravity bong was not as glamorous as it sounded. He brought out a two-liter soda bottle that was cut in half with the cap fashioned into a bowl for the marijuana and placed it in a bucket of water. He told me to "watch and learn" as he lit the cap. The bottle rose up in the water as it filled with smoke. He cleared his throat in preparation, unscrewed the cap, placed his mouth on the lip of the bottle, and sucked back a half-liter THC cloud, as the bottle top fell back into the bucket due to . . . gravity. After my first hit, I felt closer to Sir Isaac Newton than ever before. The beige futon was sinking. My skin itched and my clothes felt too tight. My head was heavy and hot, and I felt really slow and dumb, as if I were encased in half-chilled

Jell-O. Maybe everything would be better if I laid down with Dark Pony . . . or maybe I needed some chamomile tea and a banana. Instead, I wrapped my lips around the mouth of the soda bong and inhaled deeply, slipping further down the introspective rabbit hole. Now I thought about how even my nieces in Calgary owned houses with backyards. I was so behind in life. I should be in my hotel room working on a pitch for a reality show, but instead I was breathing in crack-laced pot through a Canada Dry bottle with a stoned pony boy. I needed serious help.

Dark Pony asked if I'd like to see a cool video. Yes, I need a distraction, perfect. I nodded, he smiled, and everything was okay for a moment. He put in a DVD and pressed play. I expected porn. What I got was video footage from a live Devo concert, but just the drum cam. That's right: a two-hour recording from the point of view of the drummer. Then my high little pony did the unimaginable. He reached under the futon, pulled out a pair of drumsticks, and began to air drum along. I wanted to scream, "Please Dark Pony, stop! With every second you're making it harder and harder for me to sleep with you, so could you please not air drum?!" It also dawned on me that I might be too messed up to have sex with Johnny Depp, let alone this guy. It was time to reassess and retreat. Interrupting his percussion solo, I asked if he could call me a cab. He laughed.

"There are no cabs around here. Don't worry, I'll drive you."

He excused himself to the bathroom. It was going to be okay. We'd make out tomorrow, right? I could still play like the kids, just not tonight. I was pacing myself. I had all week.

He took his time in the bathroom. I could hear running water, and it sounded like maybe he was brushing his teeth? Then I put two and two together; he was preparing for the car make out. Yes! Maybe I wasn't too fucked-up. Maybe the night was just getting started. He finally emerged, smelling slightly of mint, and it turned me on. We slid into his car, the pony express, full of potential.

As he stuck the key into the ignition, he asked, "So, I don't see a ring. Are you married?"

"No, I'm not married!" I was a little insulted, but also found it incredible that he presumed that I would cheat on my husband with him. Yeah, I'm going to throw a lifetime commitment away on a guy who plays air drums. Don't flatter yourself, buddy.

At the first red light, I took stock of the situation again. I had a small opening to make this happen. I placed a hand on his leg, he looked at me intently—*god, he was young*—and we started kissing. We both had dry mouth so it wasn't fabulous, but I did find it exhilarating. It was like robbing a bank and being told I was pretty at the same time. Hands started moving, clothes were stretching . . . and then the light turned green.

He stepped on the gas, and I noticed that I was grinning hard while staring out at the road ahead of us, trying to maximize the rush from speeding and kissing. We zipped down the empty streets, and at the next stoplight we made out again. As we sped off the second time, I noticed that red and blue lights were bouncing off the windshield. It looked beautiful. Wait a second—*why* were there red and blue lights bouncing off the windshield?

Out of the back window I could see a police car right behind us, flashing its lights for us to pull over.

"Fuck," muttered Dark Pony. "I'm going to pull over. Okay? Fuck. But it'll be cool; they have nothing on me."

Before I could ask what the hell he was talking about, a knuckle tapped on the driver's window and flashlights shone in on either side of the car. My body tensed as I realized that I couldn't remember what this guy's real name was. Dark Pony rolled down his window.

"Hello, Michael."

That's right. His name was Michael. How could I forget that name?

Wait. Why did the cop know his name?

Michael stepped out of the car, and through the window I watched him get cuffed and escorted back to the police car. This was not good. Who was this guy? What was he wanted for? What had I been smoking? I jumped out of the car onto the street with the idea that I'd walk to an intersection and find a cab. Immediately, a police officer ran toward me yelling, "Ma'am! You wait right there, ma'am!" He had a thick Southern accent, but without the charm.

"I need to get home. I need to get a cab back to my hotel!" I fake-blubbered, playing the damsel in distress.

"I need you to get back in the car, ma'am." He took me for more of a crack whore.

I froze. I didn't know what to do. I'd never been in any trouble with the cops before, except for one speeding ticket. Being from Canada I'd forgotten that pot was taken very seriously in parts of America. Didn't they refuse John Lennon at the border because of pot? And he

192 ~ SCREW EVERYONE

was a fucking Beatle! What chance did I have? Oh my god, I was going to get deported for drugs all because I didn't want to face my empty hotel room.

"Get back in the car for now, ma'am, and we'll let you know when you can go, okay?" he said, this time a little softer.

I nodded and stepped back into the car. I waited a few minutes, sweating, shaking, and feeling pathetic. I didn't even know who my one call from jail would be to. The opening act? He did give me his business card.

There was a knock on my window. It was the cop.

"Ma'am, I'm going to have to search your bag and your person."

"Why?"

The officer repeated what he was going to do, and I got out of the car.

"I'm sorry," I said while handing him my purse. He halfheartedly rummaged through it, like a rented security guard at an office building.

"I'd pat you down, but it would be hard to hide something in pants that tight." The sexist remark made me feel better. Somehow it humanized the experience, and I could tell that he was trying to be nice.

"Is he your boyfriend?"

I wanted to playfully reply, "Why do you ask, officer?" but I wasn't so sure the copper and I were ready to joke around yet.

"No, I met him tonight. I'm a comic, and he drove me home because I was drinking a lot." I wondered if he could smell the weed on me. I prayed that my Lady Mitchum Spring Rain deodorant overpowered it.

"You're a comic, huh? Are you funny?"

Really? I was going to have to prove my comedic worth to a police officer who was trying to bust me for drugs? Incredible.

"I'm just okay," I replied, with my best self-deprecating delivery. Sympathy seemed the best way to go.

"I do a show, get way too drunk, and agree to let this guy drive me home. Now I'm talking to the police at 3:00 AM. And it's only Tuesday!" I needed to make it sound like this never happens. But then I giggled, and it turned into a bout of uncontrollable giggling because of the stress and tension, and because I was STILL HIGH OUT OF MY HEAD.

"I'm really, really drunk," I said, trying to cover. One thing for sure, there was no law against being a dumb, inebriated passenger with tight pants on.

"Well, ma'am, you need to be a little bit more careful about who you drink with." He paused. "Maybe I'll try to come see your show this weekend?"

I was amazed that things had changed so drastically that I was going to offer him free tickets in exchange for my freedom.

"Yes, sir. That would be great." Please don't deport me.

"I'm going to go check on your friend here so we can figure out how we're going to get you back to your hotel. Why don't you get back in the car and wait."

I slumped back into the bucket seat, fatigued as if I'd finished an intense performance. I wanted nothing more than to go back to my shitty hotel room and bask in my loneliness.

Two minutes later the driver's door opened, and there was the dark pony—or Michael. Unshackled. He seemed relaxed, like it was all a little boring and routine for him. He didn't say a thing.

"What the hell happened?!" I demanded.

"They thought they could get me on drugs, but they didn't have anything on me so they had to let me go. Gave me a ticket for having a busted tail light. Assholes."

"They searched my bag!" I said, like I was too classy of a lady for that kind of treatment. I guess I should have thought of that when I was sucking on a gravity bong.

"Yeah, well, they didn't have anything on either of us."

Don't pull me into your weird criminal world because I kissed you.

"Man, I'm so glad I did a little meth before I left the apartment."

"What?" I looked at him for clarification. Pot was one thing, but crystal meth? Jesus. And then I got it. He didn't spend twenty minutes in the bathroom getting all pretty for me; he just wanted to snort some crystal in the comfort of his own home. Great! I felt deceived, defeated, and dehydrated.

Finally, we pulled into my hotel driveway. I was no longer stoned. I was gloomy. He put the car in park.

"I could use a drink. How about you?" Was he kidding? No. He was twenty-two.

"I think I need to go to bed."

"Oh yeah? Can I come up?"

"I think I need a break," I said as a bit of a joke, but I also meant it. This game was way into overtime. The flip-flopping all night long was too taxing: it's on, it's off, it's back on, it's the police.

I should have laid out the itinerary at the bar: "Listen, we're going to go back to your place, we'll smoke a joint, make out, have some decent foreplay, subpar sex, and then you'll drive me home before breakfast. Got it? Good. And grab two bottles of water before we leave. I get thirsty."

I kissed him good-bye, on the cheek, and seconds later I was back at my hotel room door where I'd started. Nothing much had changed except I'd made out with a meth addict and talked shop with a North Carolina cop. My self-esteem clicked one notch lower. Two more notches until "Failed Suicide Attempt." I still had some breathing room.

I slept most of the next day, and then slowly made my way to the club, hungover and looking a little rough. I said hi to the hostess as I walked in.

"I heard you had one crazy night last night," she remarked. I guess that was how this town worked: Everyone was in everyone's business. That's how it stayed exciting. I tried to order a Diet Coke from the waitress, but I couldn't seem to get her attention. Whatever.

The show started and the crowd seemed pumped, so I harnessed all the energy I had left for them. Onstage the adrenaline surged and the endorphins fired, making everything vivid and great. I started in on my dating jokes.

"I'm single, but I go on a few dates a month . . . just to remind myself that I have no standards . . . "

It got a good laugh, but I heard a female voice in the crowd say something like, "Yer fulla shit!"

Was I being heckled? Really? I searched for the heckler, and I saw that it was one of the waitresses. Impossible. But it was. My eyes focused in and there she was, standing, facing me defiantly with a tray in hand. I looked at her, she looked at me, and the audience looked at us both. I could feel the anticipation of the crowd, always hungry for a brawl. I had no idea why this was happening, but first things first: I needed a comeback.

"She's just bitter because I'm talking about her boyfriend!" I got a solid laugh, but I saw a fire ignite in her eyes as she whipped her blonde head around and walked away. I continued with my act while trying to piece it together. Why would she do that? Did she have a thing for Dark Pony or . . . Oh my god, I *was* talking about her boyfriend! Holy fuck! And now she was going to kill me. I kept telling jokes, going over my time, because I was scared stiff of what awaited me off stage. She couldn't attack me while I was still holding a microphone. The red light went from solid to flashing, signaling that it was time to wrap it up. Reluctantly, I said thank you, calmly shook the emcee's hand, and then bolted from the stage to the bathroom. It was the only place I could think of that had a door with a lock.

She came into the bathroom a few minutes later. Fuck.

"Ophelia?" she barked. Technically that wasn't my name, so I didn't have to answer. I wondered if she had a gun pointed at my faded yellow stall.

"*Uh,* yeah?" This wasn't the time to correct her.

"Never, ever come near my boyfriend again." Simple. Succinct. Super scary.

"Seriously . . . I didn't know . . . I had no idea . . . " I stammered. How did she even know about last night? Did he tell her? There was one thing for sure—they didn't live together. No woman lived in that apartment.

"Shut up. Did you hear me?"

"Yes." What was I going to say? *Don't worry, I don't really want him. I was bored and he seemed easy.* God, that pony turned out to be the furthest thing from easy. Harder to break than I ever could have imagined.

She said something else, something like "have a nice week" or "I'm going to kill you in your sleep," but I couldn't hear her over the pounding of blood in my head. However, I did hear the swooshing of the bathroom door as it swung shut. The brevity of our talk freaked me out. It made her all the more dangerous with her carefully chosen words and confident delivery. She sounded like she'd killed before. After half an hour, I quietly emerged from my stall and took a seat at the far end of the club to order my comp meal, but no one approached my table or came by to take my drink order. No one working there even glanced in my direction. Waitresses walked by and deliberately ignored me. This was her revenge. I couldn't eat, I couldn't drink. I was blown away that she had that much pull with the staff. She must do the payroll or scheduling.

The rest of the week was particularly lonely. I was invisible to the venue, hungry and parched, and Michael didn't acknowledge me at all. Half of me felt bad for the waitress—after all, Dark Pony was part of her life—and the other half thought that after what I went through, it was me who deserved sympathy. I arrived, did my set, and left. On Sunday when I got paid, it seemed like a lot less than what I thought I was getting, but I didn't say anything.

That pony ride cost me a lot. I should have hired one of those male prostitutes from the postcard; it would have been cheaper and easier. Thanks so much, Raleigh. I asked for *different*, and I got it.

CHAPTER 16

ENDLESS LASAGNA

My roommate was often out of town, so for the most part I lived alone. I used the freedom to lie around the apartment half-clothed and ponder, "If I killed myself right now, who would be the first person to find me?"

I usually came to the conclusion that it would be a tie between MasterCard and my student loan processor.

Even though I equated being with one person for the rest of my life with settling for less, all my freelancing, subletting, and casual dating made me thirst for some kind of permanence—on any level. I was beginning to think that maybe, just maybe, dating someone for, say, four months would be nice . . . or even a year, but I didn't want to be greedy. While I was getting good at the witty and biting repartee and deleting guys' phone numbers before they could call me back, I was concerned that my behavior was unsustainable, much like particleboard furniture: It's cool-looking in the beginning, functional for a few years after that, but eventually, it looks like cheap crap.

I still had plenty of time to figure it out. Right?

At least until after the weekend?

I scored a stand-up gig opening for a local headliner at a comedy club in Orange, New Jersey. Calling it a comedy club was generous—it was more of an abandoned event space in the basement of a family restaurant. The stage was a small wooden platform, like a children's sandbox turned upside down, surrounded by a bunch of scuffed and chopped banquet tables. Still, rumor had it that it was packed every weekend with intelligent, excited crowds.

I hadn't met the headliner yet—some local guy named Rob. I was prepared to react indifferently, but he made a big impression on me when he walked into the prep kitchen, a.k.a., our green room, and his first words to me were "Can you get me a Coke, please?" I was instantly offended and intrigued.

Offended because he assumed I was a waitress. Intrigued because he was pretty cute, and he did say "please." From under his baseball cap peered a pair of warm brown eyes reflecting slight damage, in an injured puppy kind of way. He looked as if he were still working out why his ex-girlfriend didn't go nuts for the spiced cranberry candle he bought her for Valentine's Day. It didn't make sense—she loved cranberries!

I said I didn't work there. I was a comic on the show. He scanned me up and down. "Oh . . . " he replied, without apology.

The lights went down and the emcee hit the stage, wooing the crowd with Ronald Reagan impressions and a handful of Michael-Jackson-is-a-pervert bits. Momentarily, I forgot what year it was. I began to get nervous that they would hate me and my autobiographical act. It didn't include even one outdated impression, not even Sean Connery. Noticing that I was wringing my hands while watching the emcee moonwalk, Rob taunted me. "Scared?"

"No!" I snapped back like a kid sister, maturing it with a get-over-yourself glare. I wanted to continue with the insulting flirty banter, but the emcee introduced me.

My set went over badly. The crowd wanted me to talk more about blow jobs, and less about my seventy-five-year-old mother sending me her first e-mail with the entire thing written in the subject line. After a strained thirty minutes of comedy—which could have been confused with giving a thoughtful speech—I left the stage to polite applause that sounded almost mocking, and I headed straight to the back bar to order a drink. The bartender bought me an Absolut and soda and toasted my set.

"You're very smart!" he said. I'd heard it a hundred times before, and it still didn't sound like "funny" to me. That being said, I was happy for the free booze and a compliment of any sort.

I gulped my cocktail, hoping it would water down my insecurities, and watched Rob bring the crowd back up with jokes that centered on being angry, bitter, and depressed. My mind wandered, obsessing about how lonely stand-up comedy could make me feel. You never have anyone to high five or commiserate with. You're in it alone. Why couldn't I have been good at improv or sketch comedy?

I wasn't looking forward to that long bus ride home, with nothing but idle time to review every excruciating detail of my pathetic life as I stared out a grimy window at the industrial wasteland that is New Jersey.

Rob's big closing joke was a really offensive, wince-inducing dog-farting joke, but the crowd howled in response. Suddenly I knew exactly how I could turn my night around. I'd resort to my fallback feel-good plan. I needed to sleep with Rob. Extra bonus: He had a car.

He left the stage to wild applause. I could tell he was pretty proud of himself, which was going to make my mission easy. I strolled into the prep kitchen and supplied the perfunctory postshow adoration. "That was great, man! Love that closer! You're like Chris Rock up there. Hey, can I catch a ride with you back to the city?"

He said, "Yeah, sure, I guess," and walked away. I assumed I should follow, and I did.

His blue Datsun was well lived-in to say the least. It took him a solid ten minutes to clear the passenger's seat of scraps of paper, balled-up T-shirts, empty food containers, and a little stuffed bear. Did he even have an apartment? As we drove, he mumbled about how he'd been miserable over the past month since some girl left him for reasons unknown, and the business had been wearing him down. He was considering meditation. Meditation? Seriously?

"You know what really calms the mind?" I said.

He looked at me with anticipation, as if I was going to reveal an important answer.

"Alcohol! Do you wanna meditate over a few drinks with me?"

He snickered and kept driving.

The Holland Tunnel felt like a corridor into a better night, a better life. It spit us out in Tribeca, and on the corner of a thin street we passed what looked like an old bar with warm orange light pouring out of its windows. It was getting late, almost last call, so we took our chances.

Once inside, I realized that we had stumbled upon "magic bar." That wasn't the name of the bar; it's when you catch a bar at its best moment, at its magic hour. The light was just low enough, dancing off the mahogany decor, to make everyone glow. The music was at the perfect level to both listen to and talk above—it was Miles Davis's *Kind of Blue*, one of my favorites. The other patrons were hip but not trendy, good-looking but not better looking than us. It was Cheers, the Regal Beagle, and the Village Vanguard rolled into one.

I ordered a martini with three olives. I liked to eat one at the beginning, one halfway through, and one at the end, as if they were rationed snacks on my hike to intoxication. Rob ordered an Amstel Light, the beer of champion lightweights. The spell of magic bar started to take hold. I found him irresistible as we conversed in a way you can only with a one-night stand. Someone you have no investment in.

"Really? Your last two girlfriends were underage? Good for you! Get 'em while they're fresh and young! Your dad's in a mental institution? Hey, not everything is genetic! Your grandfather was in the SS? What a coincidence—I *am* Jewish."

His contemptuous tone gave everything a "been there, done that" edge. He came off like a typical angry man. He wasn't apologetic, or a mama's boy, or even nice. I had to admit, I kind of liked

204 ~ SCREW EVERYONE

it. It made me feel like a delicate ray of sunshine in comparison. My brain started to do that twenty-years-in-the-future trick I despised but couldn't control. We were at our summerhouse in Barcelona, sitting on our terracotta patio, drinking espresso, waiting for our maid to bring out our paella. We shared a laugh remembering that he used to do a dog-fart joke.

It was closing time. Finally, he asked me the question I had been avoiding since I moved to Manhattan.

"Wanna come back to my place in Queens?"

I deflated. Queens was a solid twenty-minute drive away. Talk about a foreplay buzzkill. How would I get home? What subways were even out there?

Who was I kidding? We both knew I was going. I was desperate for connection, even if it was fraying, tenuous, or located in Queens. Like a junkie, when my narcotic of choice wasn't available, I took what I could get. And it was perfect timing—checkmark on the fresh bikini wax.

Although I didn't feel like going through "the scar" chat, I also wasn't afraid he'd be repulsed; it just meant reality would suddenly poke its ugly head into our night. I wouldn't be another girl anymore; I'd be that "scarred girl." It added a level of vulnerability to an experience that I wanted to be fun and purely physical. Revealing the scar meant revealing myself. Could I just leave my shirt on? Yeah, *that* would be normal.

Twenty minutes later, we arrived at the house where he lived. We crept down the brown sisal-rug stairs to his bachelor pad in the basement of a Greek family's home. His place wasn't terrible; it was clean, and there was even a minimal attempt at decor: a coffee table with a magazine on it and a framed picture of a sports car. However, the vase of silk flowers standing on a rattan end table didn't make any sense. They were so out of place that I couldn't help but think there was a webcam stashed in the bud of a rose.

Time was running out, and I was filled with anxiety over the stupid scar situation. He was about to open his bedroom door when I blurted out, "Okay, there's something I have to tell you."

"All right," he replied cautiously. "What's up?"

"*Uhhhh . . .* " I gave him a goofy smile to try to lighten up the dramatic moment I'd accidentally created.

"Okay, well, *uhhh*, I'll get to it. Sorry I'm making this so weird!"

"What's going on?" He was completely lost.

"Okay, I was in a bad car accident when I was a kid, and I have a huge scar on my stomach, so don't be freaked out. I'm totally fine, and it doesn't hurt or anything—it's just a big scar. See?!" I lifted up my shirt while sucking in my stomach to make it look as flat as possible. I was embarrassed by my own explanation. I may as well have said, "Want to see my boo-boo?"

He laughed a little. "Jesus, you built it up so much I thought you were going to say you had a tail or something." He came closer to examine it and ran his finger lightly down the center of my torso.

"I like that scar. It's cool. You've been through something."

Good. That was the response I'd hoped for. I was ready to resume the seduction.

"Now, I have something special to show you," he said flirtatiously and swung open the unfinished wooden door to his bedroom.

In that one moment before light revealed the inner contents of his boudoir, I envisioned many things. Another man? A harness? A bunk bed?

To say I was stunned by the actual contents would be putting it lightly. It was like nothing I had ever seen before, especially from a grown man, or at least one in the same room with me. Rob's room was full of—and I mean *covered* with—Garfields. Stuffed ones, ceramic ones, bronze ones, Garfields in a variety of poses on a special Garfield-only shelf. There was Golfing Garfield, Pool Hall Garfield, Garfield *avec un beret*, and Angry Garfield. Plus a huge one, twice the size of me, adorned with Mardi Gras beads, propped up on his bed. There were so many of them, frozen in orange-and-black-striped action, it was chilling. I didn't quite get it. If I performed well, would I win one?

The sight of this altar to Jim Davis's dynasty killed any sexy, warm, or even *safe* feeling. He was way more scarred than I could ever be. Then I had what I refer to now as a *Kaiser Soze* moment, where I reflected on our night, the things he said, and started to connect the dots. The dog-fart joke, the stuffed bear in his car, the fact that he dated much younger girls, that weird comment about my having a tail . . . Since I didn't have a coffee cup, my jaw dropped.

"*Um* . . . well . . . how did . . . what's up with all the Garfields?" I asked. I knew I should at least show him the same acceptance he did for me, but he was thirty-seven years old for god's sake! Clearly he hadn't gone through anything.

"Oh, I've had them since college," he explained, tossing it off as if amassing a huge stuffed animal collection was a perfectly normal collegiate activity. I was hoping for more of a *They were left to me by my sweet crazy aunt when she died, and I have to display them to keep my inheritance,* or even, *They're a childhood collection that is now worth millions!*

My mind flashed again to our conversation at the bar. He mentioned he was from Boston, that he'd gone to Boston U, then moved to Providence for a while, and then moved back to Boston, then to Manhattan, then to Brooklyn, and now Queens. All I could picture was him wrapping each precious Garfield in newspaper and gently placing them in a cardboard liquor box time after time. I felt cheated and a little ill. He wasn't a sexy man; he was a fucked-up man-child. To top it off, I was in Queens.

I tried to work with the situation. "Can you take a few of them out of your room? They're creeping me out a little." He did, without question, almost as if he had done it before for other trapped desperate girls who were trying anything to make the love den less infantile. He removed the big cat from the bed and carefully selected two other ones from the top of his dresser, setting them neatly on the sofa in the next room. When he returned, he flung me onto the bed and pounced. At least the Garfields were working their magic on one of us.

Turns out the only thing bigger than his Garfield obsession was his penis. It made perfect sense. Only a thirty-seven-year-old guy with a dick that big could get away with a bedroom full of stuffies. I had never seen one *that* big before and wasn't sure how to approach it. It looked fake, or like it could strangle me. I'm sure he nicknamed it Odie. Without warning, he threw on a Magnum condom and just . . . stuck it in.

The next thing I knew we were having the world's worst, most unskilled sex I had ever experienced. Basically, he lowered his head beside my right ear and pumped furiously like a jackhammer. Like Odie in heat. It took a few moments for me to even catch up to what was happening. It felt like he was punching me inside. Like he was fucking a stuffed Garfield, and not even the favorite in his collection. I imagined that under his bed, I would find a bounty of old, mutilated, sticky orange-and-black cats.

More important, had he ever been with a woman before? What past girlfriend would put up with this? Even with all my problems and baggage, I knew that my scar and I were way above this. The sex was so empty and mechanical that I actually started making life resolutions in my head. *Tomorrow, I'm going to go to the gym, cut down on the drinking, stick to a disciplined writing schedule, get out of debt, get a better apartment . . . Tomorrow is a brand new day. I still have my whole life ahead of me. It's not too late.*

I turned to look at him—at least I could do my job—but his eyes were shut. He had a tight smile on his face as he continued to thrust at a sprinter's pace. He was lost in some fantasy world. A world of no Mondays and endless lasagna.

And then it was over. He rolled off and wiped perspiration from his forehead. I felt like I had been duped by a distracted carny running a crappy and dangerous ride at the county fair.

"Do you want me to go down on you or something?"

Yeah, *or something*, I thought.

"No . . . I'm good." I smiled with fake reassurance. Bad missionary-style sex is one thing. Bad oral sex would be unbearable. I didn't feel motivated to give him useful tips and guidance. Let the next girl deal with it.

He actually wanted to cuddle, and I let him. He wasn't bad at it. Clearly this was more in his wheelhouse. Emotion swelled in my body as he spooned me tight, and I was surprised that I had to choke back tears. Tomorrow was a brand new day.

CHAPTER 17

TURN AROUND, BRIGHT EYES

M y dear old friend and drinking buddy, Lisa, was visiting from Toronto, and we met up at a French brasserie where I was a regular, yet the staff never seemed to recognize me. Either it was part of the joint's charm, or they were really trying to be authentically French. I always ordered the same drink, what the menu called "Country White Wine," which was a fancy way of saying "the cheapest one." On this particular Wednesday night, I changed things up and asked for a Grey Goose vodka on the rocks with a lemon. Why? Because I was on a downward spiral, and tossing back a half glass of fruity white wine wasn't going to cut it. I wanted that feeling of thick alcohol sliding down my throat, coating the ball of confusion and pain in my gut. The lemon on the side was to camouflage its utilitarian purpose: to make it look like I was festively cocktailing. A word to the wise: If you ever meet me, and I order a vodka on the rocks, just know that it means I'm on the rocks too.

Lisa hugged me warmly, ordered herself a cosmo (because she was in New York!), and asked me to tell her about everything that was going on. I tried my best to make it all sound hilarious and upbeat, but as the words came out of my mouth, they sounded brutally sad.

"The dating scene is pretty intense here. I went out with a ridiculously good-looking guy, but he turned out to be a cocaine addict. Hilariously, he's the one still calling me. There's been a comic here, and a married guy there . . . Oh, and get this: A guy actually told me how he likes his girls waxed. I was like, 'Is that an acrylic sweater you're wearing? Yeah, you don't get a choice!'"

Lisa looked more concerned than entertained, so I continued.

"But the best one of all just happened. After this gig a couple Fridays ago, I went home with the headliner, who proudly showed me his bedroom full of . . . stuffed Garfields! Ta-da! Seriously, Lisa, everyone in this town is insane. At least with that guy, if it worked out, we could donate the Garfields to a children's charity."

I could tell that Lisa was judging me. Unbelievable. She was the woman who slept with married men; she was the girl who polished off a pitcher of beer and then went home to work on her thesis. She was a fellow independent woman whose life goals didn't include settling down. She was my idol. And now she was judging me.

Lisa calmly put down her cosmo before she spoke, mostly because it's impossible to make a serious point with a pink cocktail in your hand. "Sounds a little out of control to me. Are you . . . *okay?*"

Her spidey senses were onto something. The bad disconnected sex with The Stuffed Feline Wonder had thrown me off my axis. I understood it was a one-night stand, and I was initially the one who didn't even want to show him the scar, but the total absence of intimacy coupled with being fucked like I was a prop had really affected me. I mean, I barely needed to be there. I was losing my patience for being of such low value.

"No no no. It's New York. It's hard to explain what's considered normal here. Don't worry, I'm fine."

If you ever hear yourself adamantly declare that you're fine, you'll immediately hear how *not fine* you really are.

"Maybe you should take a break from chasing such a big life," she suggested.

"Heeeyyy," I said, slurring already. "I'm doing the best I can with what's out there. Plus, I already wrote a joke about the Garfield guy. Did I mention he had a massive penis? I think he said its name was Odie."

Lisa didn't laugh along. The fact that our catch-up had suddenly turned into a mini-intervention worried me. Wasn't I operating like anyone else? Did I really seem out of control?

I ordered another Grey Goose. Rocks. Lemon.

"Is there anyone that you like? A guy from work or . . . someone else in the comedy world? Have you thought about Internet dating?"

Internet dating was still new, and although I didn't subscribe to the stigma others had placed on it, I'd been around the block enough times to title my profile "As Is." I was definitely done dating within the comedy scene. My track record was abysmal, and the thought of falling asleep beside someone who turns off the light and asks, "So why do you think my Wal-Mart joke doesn't work anymore?" totally repelled me.

But there was one guy, not in the comedy scene, whom I was interested in.

"There is this Jonathan guy."

"Well, can you get in touch with that Jonathan guy?" asked Lisa innocently.

"Yeah, probably," I said into my drink. "But he's probably a douche."

"Ah, c'mon. You wouldn't be attracted to him if he was like that."

I felt like a washed-up Broadway ingenue, and I wanted to yell, "What do you know, Lisa? You have health care and rational men. It's different here in the Big Apple, sweetheart!"

This Jonathan guy was a new employee at the company where Allison, one of my closest comedy friends, worked. He came to our show, and I say *came to our show* lightly. More accurately, we bullied him and his two guy friends into buying tickets to our show.

Allison and I ran a weekly stand-up show in the basement of a West Village bar, and when we didn't have enough of an audience, we'd head out to the street and try to persuade passersby to come in, a process known as "barking in a crowd." In hindsight, I can't believe it worked at all. It was pretty demoralizing to stand on the street as grown women with college degrees and beg random people to come see our little dog-and-pony show. Maybe the strangers found us cute or felt sorry for us, or maybe they thought we were the worst prostitutes ever. Whatever it was, we would miraculously scare up a full room every time.

Jonathan and his pals were three of those suckers whom I lured in with the promise of "a few laughs from a handful of New York's top comics, cheap booze, and an overall good time." I didn't know any of their names at the time; I didn't even know he worked with Allison. The thing that stuck with me was that one of them had these big brilliant-blue eyes. Like a wolf's eyes. I remembered that pair of eyes beaming up at me from the audience—which was unusual. I had a knack for scanning a room full of faces and ignoring the happy smiling ones to locate the person having the worst time. Every other last audience member could be laughing, cheering, having the time of their life, but I'd hone in on the man or woman who looked miserable, and then I'd spend the rest of my act delivering my material straight to them in some sort of twisted Mexican joke standoff. They were the only ones who mattered. More often than not, those same people would approach me after the show to say thank you and that they had a good time.

I wasn't used to the idea of a guy flirting with me from the audience, either. A lot of men get into comedy not only because they are funny but also because it's a sure ticket to getting laid. It doesn't quite happen the same way for female comics. Why? When have you ever heard a guy say, "I'm looking for a girl with a great sense of humor—and if she is funnier than me, well, that would be such a turn-on!"

After my Canadian intervention, I asked Allison if she could find out if Jonathan wanted to go for a drink with me.

"Jonathan . . . okay." Allison hesitated. "I was going to set him up with someone else."

"Well, see if after that someone else, he wants to go for a drink with me. But make sure it's him."

I'd already gone on a date with Jonathan, or so I'd thought, but it turned out to be one of the other guys in the group. As I mentioned, I didn't know any of their names, but I received an e-mail from Daryl. He said that he loved my set and asked if I'd like to "rendezvous for a couple of pints." Sure, he was mixing French and British words, but at least it showed an attempt at originality. I suggested we meet at my favorite restaurant at the time, a high-volume, chaotic Chinese place called Congee Village. Looking back, that place was almost like an obstacle course for a first date, but I loved the food, there was no "scene" to have to fit into, and their drinks were strong and cheap.

I waited on an orange Lucite stool in the bar area of Congee Village, not entirely sure who I was looking for. All I remembered were the eyes—eyes that I saw from the stage, not even close up. I was pretty sure that all three of the guys had brownish hair, and beyond that I hoped that I would just intuitively know when he walked in. The place was 99 percent Asian, so it was bound to be easy. Unless he was Asian. With blue eyes.

But then I saw him. Unmistakable. It wasn't because of those big sparkling eyes; it was more that he stuck out, like a clumsy lost child, sporting a huge backpack like he'd come straight from Cub Scout camp. As soon as bright eyes turned around, I realized there had been a mistake. Yes, he had eyes, two of them, but they were brown, and tucked behind a pair of dirty glasses with tape on the frame. He wasn't bright eyes.

There was no way to say, "There's been a misunderstanding," without insulting him. As far as he knew, things were going exactly as planned. I could tell two things right away: The menu frightened him, and he didn't go out on a lot of dates. To be fair, the Congee Village menu was a bit daunting. It included a lot of fowl's organs, snails, and strange fish. He gagged at the sight of the cold jellyfish appetizer I ordered (delicious, although you have to get over the fact that it looks like a pile of cut-up rubber bands with chili flakes on top), and he absolutely refused to try it. The only thing he would eat was a basic chicken and rice dish, which I categorized as a character flaw. I couldn't tell if he was tripping over his words because he was worried about how our first date was going, or if that was just the way he talked, but it was a problem. To be fair, he had a lot of interesting things to say, things that I had no interest in. I didn't know anything about comic books beyond Betty and Veronica, and I wasn't into movie trivia. Why? Because I wasn't a nerd boy.

"So . . . but . . . do you have a . . . what's your favorite movie?" he asked.

"That's easy. *Raiders of the Lost Ark,* hands down. And basically I've tried to model my entire life after Marion. Speaking of which, do you wanna do a shot?" My eyes lit up when I said *shot.* Not because I was chasing some spring-break-in-Miami dragon; I was just excited at the idea of introducing something that might help take the parking brake off our date.

"*Uh* . . . nooo . . . I don't think so . . . shots and me . . . *heh heh* . . . not a good idea."

218 ~ SCREW EVERYONE

I gave him a phony smile and inwardly sighed. Of course they're not a good idea. Shots are never a good idea—THAT'S THE POINT. Shots serve one purpose only: to lose control. The check came, and of course, we split it. I didn't even blame him for not trying to pay—this wasn't a date; it was an error. I was dying to know if his backpack was full of camping equipment, comic books, or a homemade, fully functioning lightsaber. My money was on the lightsaber.

We did one of those far-apart hugs good-bye, and I turned down the next street and texted the coke guy, even though I'd programmed his number in as "DO NOT PICK UP." I asked him if he wanted to meet for . . . another drink. Anything to override the past couple of hours. He said he'd be there in half an hour. I entered a new bar and ordered a Grey Goose on the rocks. These guys were all such idiots.

A FEW WEEKS later, Allison told me that she gave Jonathan my number. He insisted that he couldn't possibly ask me out on a date for two reasons: one, there was some sort of guy honor code stating that you couldn't go out with a girl your friend had already dated, and two, he wasn't into actresses. From his past experiences, all performers were overly dramatic, narcissistic, and difficult. When she told me this, I rolled my eyes. First of all, I'd barely dated his friend and motioned that our missed-connection dinner be removed from both of our records, immediately. Second, I can't act. I didn't have high enough self-esteem to be a decent narcissist. He was making excuses because he wasn't into me. What was I going to do—force him to meet up with me so he could reject me in person? She claimed that she threw my phone number at him and said, "Call her. It's just a drink!"

Who wouldn't respond to that?

A few days later, I was nursing a latte and a water and working out my comedy set, when my cell phone rang. It displayed a number I didn't recognize, so naturally I let it go to voice mail. It turned out to be Jonathan, calling to set up a date. I guess he finally got clearance from Daryl and was willing to take a chance on the high-maintenance performer. Yet on his message he sounded energetic and authentically interested in meeting up. Whatever. I was already over bright eyes. He was probably super boring. Then again, maybe he'd pay for my drinks. Even I wasn't crazy about the cynic I was turning into.

I called him back, not allowing myself to flirt with optimism for one second, and scrolled through the possibilities of what this guy would be into that I couldn't predict. Did he have a creepy sex fetish? Was he in love with his mother? Passionate about pregnant porn? Gay? By the time we met up, how many dates would he have already gone on that week? Fifteen? Would he have one with me at 7:00 PM and another lined up at 10:00 PM, with a booty call on speed dial if need be? Good. So would I. I didn't know with whom, but I'd figure that out. I was immune to this stuff. I could *use* just as much as I could be *used*. I called him back, and he picked up. Wow. Amateur move. No one picked up their phone anymore. The conversation was a little wooden, but we set up a date for drinks at a little Italian snack bar in a couple of days. In preparation I decided to go to the gym. Once.

When I arrived, on time, Jonathan was already there, waiting outside. He was definitely the guy with the eyes, and they were just as stunning. At least we got that right. He greeted me warmly, with an inviting laugh, gave me a half hug/half pat on the back, and complimented me on my long red skirt. He had some interesting facial hair going on, inspired in part by Johnny Depp's beard du jour: a small mustache and a small soul patch and a small goatee. I don't know what it was called, but with his short-cropped, almost black hair, it made him look a bit swarthy. I didn't mind it. At least there was grooming. It wasn't quite Captain Jack Sparrow, but it was a Jewish, New Yorky version of Johnny Depp.

Jonathan Depp.

His button-down shirt was bursting with colors and had beads sewn on as part of the pattern. I will say they were the best use of beads I'd seen on a men's shirt not sold in a Halloween costume store, but they were still beads. And I knew, more than anyone, that there was no such thing as masculine beads. I wasn't judging him as much as I was doing detective work, observing and trying to interpret the evidence. Every little thing could give me insight as to who this guy was and help me avoid a bedroom full of Garfields. What did a beaded shirt mean? He said he bought it in Montreal. Having lived in Montreal, I understood how it might have worked there, the same way that you might excuse a bolo tie in Wyoming or New Mexico . . . but in New York? Then again, as a former employee of Beadworks, I let it go and we continued.

Much like his friend Daryl, Jonathan seemed oddly nervous. I figured it was because he was hiding something twisted. Soon I'd find out what. I ordered a bottle of wine, but he suggested we hold off and start with a glass each. A bottle, he said, was "a big commitment."

Well, if you can't commit to a bottle of wine . . .

I played my usual game, kept the conversation going, nice and light, and I insulted him a bit, like we were children in grade school who didn't know yet how to express desire, and waited for him to hit the ball back. But he didn't respond to the emotionally cavalier character I'd constructed. He didn't want to do biting banter. He was actually very normal, telling me about his new job and asking me about life in Canada. Unfortunately, like Daryl, he was also a comic book nerd, but at least he was good-looking. That was a winning combination: low self-esteem but attractive. I'd finished my glass of wine and sarcastically asked permission to order another. He laughed and said, "Yeah, why not?"

I wasn't sure about this guy. He seemed to be the most regular person I'd come across in two years, minus the beaded shirt. But we seemed to be having a pretty good time. I mean, it wasn't fireworks, but it was oddly comfortable. It was also clear that he hadn't endured as many relationships and hook-ups as I had, which was actually refreshing. He was a bit of a lightweight in the boyfriend boxing ring. Or at least that's what he presented. There was a distinct possibility he was a mirage, a charmer, an emotional con man.

We finished up and he paid, even though I could tell he did it very reluctantly, checking every line item carefully on the bill before throwing down cash. It was 9:00 PM and I was up for more, so I invited him out for another drink. What the hell? I told him I'd pay, to even things out.

He said, "I'd like that." Not exactly the right answer, but enough to move forward.

At the second bar, I made a big production about ordering a bottle of wine, that I could handle the length of that relationship, and halfway through it I started to feel . . . drunk. I was ready to challenge things a little. Let's see how a *real* conversation goes. I leaned in and said in my best faux seductive voice, "So, Jonathan. Tell me. What do you want out of life?"

He thought about it and answered honestly. "Jeez. Okay. Well, I'd like to get married some day, buy an apartment, have kids, you know . . . "

But I didn't.

"I don't want any of those things," I snapped, while empting my glass. "Other than the apartment."

"Really? You don't want to get married?"

I gave him an irritated look. Maybe all those other actresses he dated wanted to get hitched; maybe narcissists were crazy about weddings. But not me. I couldn't wait to set him straight.

"No, I don't. You have to be an idiot to want to get married—unless of course there is land or a huge inheritance involved. Why would anyone be stupid enough to get married? It's an old-fashioned and failed institution. Most marriages end in divorce. What's the point?" God, had I been giving that same speech since high school?

He looked at me, a bit dazed. It was time to switch gears. I was getting deep in my cups and wanted some action. I didn't feel like waiting any longer for him to make the first move. So I threw myself at him. I grabbed him and started kissing him. He didn't refuse, push away, or even mildly hesitate, and the make out was pretty good, for a late, intoxicated, public make out. It found its natural closure when the waitress laid down the bill.

I paid while giving Jonathan a look that I could tell he didn't have the faintest clue how to interpret. Thankfully, I was a few blocks away from my apartment, and I wasn't about to ask him back. I needed to mull over the whole thing. He cut me off at the pass and asked where he could grab a cab to get back to Brooklyn. He had to work tomorrow. Somehow, I ended up walking him to a taxi, where he gave me a quick peck on the mouth and zoomed away, leaving me standing on the sidewalk. He probably should have offered to walk me home, no? So I did what I did best—I walked myself home.

When he called me the next day, I instinctively hit *Ignore*. I wasn't falling for whatever shit he was pulling, and I didn't need to hear how he had a great time but it turns out his girlfriend was back in town, or it was going to be really busy at work for the next few weeks, *but we'll be in touch*. It was none of that. Instead, his voice mail was simple, stating that he'd been thinking about me all day and would love to go on another date. I blushed through my bitterness, smiled through my skepticism, waited half a day to make sure that I wanted to do this, and finally called him back. He asked if I wanted to go see a movie the next night. Weird.

CHAPTER 18

THE LAST COMEDIENNE

O n my second date with Jonathan, I excused myself from kissing on my couch to top off our cabernets. While unscrewing the bottle, I took a moment to acknowledge how rare it had become to date a guy who didn't come with a glaring drug problem, mental illness, or a wife. He wasn't acting cool, making himself out to be a player, rushing us into the bedroom, or spending the evening listening to the sound of his own voice. I'm sure he had tons of other problems—for instance, he mentioned that he sang in a barbershop quartet, and had never used the word *sorry* in practice—but from what I could tell, he was the kind of human who gave humans a good name.

He claimed to have old-fashioned values in that 1990s way— looking for a nice, stable girlfriend, the goal being contentment. I wasn't sure if I qualified. I'd made too many hard choices along the way to cash in my one chip and happily move to a subdivision, buy

Luna bars in bulk at Costco, fantasize about hiring a landscaper, and pop out an acceptable number of entitled offspring. I didn't even want to "check in" with someone if I changed my plans. My longest relationship was with comedy, and it still had priority over everything else. I knew the third time I apologized for missing his best friend's birthday party or his brother's wedding because I had three non-paying spots and needed to drop by this new club to meet the booker, there would be a fight.

Sure I yearned for all the good stuff: affection, companionship, someone to list as my emergency contact. I didn't even mind the idea of exclusivity. At least if we had sex for a while, we could build on a skill set. But how long would it take before we became another shitty couple in a coma of complacency, silently staring at menus in a restaurant, no longer worried that if I ordered the steak and he paid, I'd be expected to put out?

Instinctively wiping the smudged black liner from under my eyes, I picked up our red wine IKEA goblets and thought, *But there is no need to stop the momentum now. I'm having fun. People are allowed to have fun, right? I'll deal with it as we go along.* The glass wasn't half-full, but it was still refillable.

And we went along, for months. He kept calling and texting, and I kept responding. Never once did I toy with the idea of renaming his contact "Don't Pick Up," or "Gah!" We joked that we were on a month-to-month lease and would check in at the end of thirty days to see if we both wanted to renew. Ah, hilarious New York real estate humor. Although it was all very promising, I'd be lying if I said that

I wasn't on guard. My shields were up, and I didn't totally trust what was going on. I've always been a doomsday thinker. If anything goes exceedingly well, I brace myself for the fall. With my budding relationship with Jonathan, I thought, *No matter what, the coke guy will take me back.* He was my equivalent of a job at McDonald's. Call it pessimistic, paranoid, pathological, or see it as I did: an intelligent approach based on experience. Why set yourself up for disappointment when you can be disappointed now?

I kept waiting for the other shoe to drop, searching for a sign that he wasn't really the combination of the contradictions he presented. Could he actually be a moral, loyal guy who was good-looking and still in his thirties? Was it possible that he loved going to musical theater yet never missed a boxing match? Did he have the garden variety of problems that I could handle? Were there no Garfields in his closet?

Jonathan shared an apartment in Williamsburg with his best friend from college and his younger brother. Williamsburg was on the cusp of blowing up into a mini metropolis of hipsters prancing around in long johns and stilettos. A year into our dating relationship, his apartment's lease was up and decisions needed to be made. Even though the guy crawled into a fetal position at the mention of housecleaning, he was very capable and mature in other ways. Jonathan was very money-conscious and had saved his shekels since his Bar Mitzvah with the hope of someday buying a starter home in New York. And suddenly he found it on the Lower East Side. It was 350 square feet. A starter closet.

Not only was it was tiny, but a fifth floor walk-up in a co-op half-populated with people who'd bought their apartments for a dollar when the landlord skipped town in the early eighties, and half who purchased their slice in the sky for at least two hundred thousand times that. The space needed to be gutted, renovated, and painted. The front metal door had a huge dent in it leftover from the battering ram the SWAT team used in a drug bust before the neighborhood gentrified. They must have been selling hospital-grade cocaine to make buyers want to climb all those stairs. But that tiny dirty hovel was Jonathan's chance to get in the game and own property in Manhattan. He put in an offer with the vague understanding that we would live there together, as the only way he could afford it was to share it with someone. And because there was hardly enough room for one full-size bed, it had to be someone like me.

We talked about the whole thing very logically and unemotionally. *Think of all the money we'd save! No more late-night cab or subway rides to be together!* We were both in our thirties, we weren't going anywhere, and this was the natural progression of a relationship. It wasn't the most exciting way to discuss a major step, using the "hey, we're getting old and it's probably not going to get any better than this, so we might as well give it a shot" rationale, but it was also . . . true. After we shacked up, we could work on our living wills.

Whether it was subconscious or not, I put up all kinds of resistance. For instance, I hated the fact that Jonathan was an extremely picky eater. I grew up in a household where having an adventurous palate was a source of pride. It made you a strong, well-rounded person. Alternatively, someone who was very particular about his food was spoiled and weak and wouldn't survive the apocalypse. Natural selection should weed them out. Jonathan's food groups were limited to meat, and meat on bread. I confronted him one night and told him that "this picky eating thing" was a deal breaker. How could I be seriously involved with someone whom I couldn't share a dinner with? Would I end up cheating on him so I could enjoy a foodie tasting menu with someone? Besides, if something so fundamental as our palates were incompatible, maybe we were too?

Jonathan listened to my rant and came up with a solution. He offered to try any food I offered him for one year and see what happened, but he still had the right to not like something. It was hard to argue with that proposal, and to test his seriousness I immediately handed him a fistful of cilantro. He picked off a leaf and chewed it, making a face like I'd given him a spoonful of caterpillar snot. But he wasn't going to roll over and be told what to do. He countered that he'd like to see some improvements on my end, especially with respect to my phone habits. He pointed out that whenever I was out I never called him when I said I would. He was right: I had a terrible tendency of getting caught up with whatever I was doing, be it a show or hanging out with other comics, and I wouldn't call.

"I don't want to be that person who has to check in all the time," I argued.

"Well," Jonathan said, "you're not single anymore, so stop treating it like you are. You can go outside for a second to call me." I bristled at the idea that my status had changed and now I had to be accountable, but he wasn't being unreasonable.

THE DAY WE moved in together, we had a huge battle about "stuff." My mother's warning that "you never really know someone until you live with them" echoed in my head. Jonathan grew up in New York, so he had his entire life's possessions with him, and by that I mean the hood ornament off his first car, seventy million comics, and one action figure. In other words, garbage. I, on the other hand, was a transient hobo with no furniture and only a couple of plants. My boxes were filled with old notebooks and clothes. And we had one closet. I watched Jonathan hoist a taped-shut banker's box onto the top shelf of *our* closet.

"What's in the box?" I inquired.

"My stuff."

"Really? That's your response? 'My stuff'? Do you really think the best way to start life living together is to have boxed secrets?"

Jonathan turned very serious.

"This is my stuff, and you are not allowed to look in the box."

I glared at him with daggers in my eyes.

"You'll find out when the time is right, okay?" he said.

What the hell did that mean? One day in the future he'd finally feel comfortable enough to break out his collection of barnyard sex tapes? No, it couldn't just be porn. It had to be way worse—like a collection of ex-girlfriends' severed heads. And that would be horrifying—especially if they were prettier than me.

The whole thing did not sit well, and I was convinced that this secret box was a red flag signaling that things would rapidly decline in our relationship.

But that didn't happen. Eventually we put our stuff away, Jonathan continued to hate tomatoes, and I often forgot to call him after shows. Yet things pleasantly rolled forward, albeit over a slightly rocky road.

Living together in such a tiny space had its own set of challenges. When we were both home, we moved around each other like Tetris pieces. I couldn't even look at normal decorating magazines because the spaces they featured were massive. I had to resort to buying boating magazines. Whenever a friend or family member braved the five flights of stairs, they'd ask the same series of stupid questions that always included, "Do you have to do this every day?," then gasp and state, "If you can stay together living here, you can do anything." I had no idea that the divorce rate was lower in mansions. Our lives were on full display to each other, and we didn't like everything we saw. It was harder to hide bleaching my mustache, or my obsessive need to clean as procrastination. I hated witnessing the insane amount of time Jonathan spent watching TV, and he seemed to leave a trail of papers, sweaty clothes, and body hair behind him. A shirt left on the floor was stealing one-tenth of our available space. But in the grand scheme of things, it was no big deal. I started to wonder if good matches weren't based so much on what you had in common with someone, but rather whose crap you could best stomach. Internet dating sites should stop asking people to sell the best version of themselves and instead prompt everyone to post their most unflattering photo and list their worst qualities. Is mean to waiters? Pass. Has unresolved anger issues? Who doesn't? Is stockpiling weapons in a secret location in case the Republicans don't win the next election? Sounds like a hobby that might get in the way. Is in love with his sister? Not my favorite, but dealable.

As it turned out, Jonathan and I fought over dirty dishes, not emotional unavailability.

I'd always sneered at his use of *content* to sum up a good relationship, but for the first time, I saw the word differently. There was comfort in coming home to someone I actually liked—even if our miniature apartment was a mess because of him. Still, I didn't have full confidence in the situation, and I never looked in the box, because I didn't want to know what was in it. Ignorance may not be bliss, but it is way easier.

Every January, like a good, young, hip Jew, Jonathan took a pilgrimage to Key West, Florida, to visit a childhood friend. Not only was this woman brilliant enough to figure out that you can live in Key West, but she also had a guest room in her apartment like a real person. I was working as a twentieth-century plumber, a.k.a., IT consultant, mostly wiping people's computers clean of viruses they caught while downloading copious amounts of porn, and I wasn't given much time off. As an assistant promo producer at a real company, Jonathan had proper vacation days, sick days, personal days, moving days, all of which added up to a lot of days. But I was in higher demand.

He flew down on Wednesday, and I'd join him on the weekend. As roommates with benefits, we didn't share money: Jonathan worried that my instability would tarnish his perfect credit score, and I didn't want anyone to think *they owned me*, so we functioned as monetary singles. Since tickets to Key West were expensive, I opted for a cheap flight to Miami and rented a car for the four-hour drive down to the last Key.

Before I left, I called and asked Jonathan if he wanted me to bring him anything. He requested some computer files. He'd just started writing his own autobiographical comics and wanted to work on the script. Knowing him, he was hogging his friend's computer, and I suggested that I copy over his whole My Documents file to my laptop and bring that down. I could do anything. I was a computer consultant.

Rushed as usual and leaving everything to the very last minute, I networked his computer to my laptop to speed up the transfer. This was before you could shove in a 64GB memory stick or drag it to Dropbox. I used physical cables. It was pretty sexy. There was the added complication that his computer ran Windows 2000, and my laptop was state of the art with Windows XP. The naming conventions of files changed between those operating systems, so while the transfer took place, any file with a weird or long name would trigger a pop-up window suggesting a new name for the file and asking if you'd like to *Accept* or *Ignore*. I sat there fuming, clicking *Accept* over and over again. I was going to miss my plane because of Jonathan's stupid files with ridiculous names. No good IT deed goes unpunished.

That was until a file popped up called "All Girls I've Ever Been With."

Storm clouds gathered over my workspace as I contemplated what to do next. As someone who has had her diary read, I knew how wrong and damaging it was to look at other people's private stuff. Reading this file would be not only an invasion of his privacy but also an admission that I didn't trust him. It would be undisputed betrayal. So I hit *Accept*, finished the transfer, and hailed a cab to the airport.

Yeah, right. We all know that didn't happen. I double-clicked that file open within two seconds of reading its name. Jonathan didn't get to have a secret file and a secret box. I needed to know who this guy really was.

Anger pulsed through my veins. The contents of the document precisely reflected its name. It was a very comprehensive list of all the girls Jonathan had been with in his life. Fifty-four in all. Not had sex with, but had been with . . . ever. There were notes beside some of them: big boobs, bad kisser, great blow job, nice underwear, liked to touch herself. I looked at each name, each bullet point, my temperature rising as my eyes scanned. At the end of the list, at number fifty-four, was my name, and beside it, just "Comedienne."

I wanted to punch the screen. The only reason I didn't was because that laptop was the most expensive thing I owned.

This was it. The evidence. A disgusting list reducing old girlfriends and experiences to their physical attributes or sexual tendencies. There were no notes beside any of these poor girls' names that said, "totally related, had great talks, super intelligent," or how about "funny"?! No, there were just misogynist asshole things about boobs and dick sucking. I was going to make it my fucking job to make sure Jonathan never got his dick sucked again. He'd be begging for the sloppy blow job of Sonja, number twenty-seven. And you know why number seventeen liked touching herself? Because you couldn't get her off—you jerk.

And then there was "comedienne." That was unforgivable. No one says "comedienne" anymore. It's derogatory, and it falls under the same category as "spinster," a long-discarded sexist term. It's "comic," or "comedian," much like how "spinster" has been replaced with "career woman" or "cougar."

Stand-up is hard enough. I didn't also need a special soft consonant name to further make me feel like I was the short-bus version of an actual comic. Like you'd see a poster for a show advertising four comics and one comedienne. *Aw—how adorable—they got a comedienne!* If I had to get in front of the same drunk, obnoxious audience as everyone else, I wanted to be called the same name.

I hated that there was a list, period. Seeing my name among a bunch of other failed experiences only made it worse. I wanted to believe that somehow I was different from the rest, the exception, much like how I tried to convince myself that he was more evolved than the other guys. Nope. He was just another dumb guy. Who keeps a list like that? I didn't, but then again I couldn't remember half the people I kissed or had oral sex with. And then there were many that I'd like to forget.

The last thing I wanted was to ever see that asshole again, which would be a major problem since we lived together. I couldn't tell him over the phone—how would that work? I'd move out before he got back? That would not be satisfying enough. No, I wanted to confront him in person. Throw my findings right in his face. Who cares that I was ruining his vacation? He'd ruined my life.

I spent the whole flight staring at the seat tray in front of me, questioning everything. How did I not see who this guy really was?

Was our love really that blinding? Why didn't he write anything about my underwear? Those lace thongs were really nice!

It was a shame to be so distraught while driving on the most beautiful one hundred miles of highway in the country. The road felt as if it were hovering over the Atlantic Ocean or suspended by the clouds, as you crossed over from one tropical island to the next. I would look out the windows and gasp at the scenery, then return to planning Mission Delete Jonathan. My idea was to start by telling him that he could take me off his stupid list and wishing him luck finding a girl who fit in better among the Sarahs and Laurens. I'd tell him he didn't deserve my great blow job that I actually cared about giving to him. Then I'd turn on my heels, drive back to the airport, and get on the next flight. After packing up my stuff, I would move to LA. Fuck that guy—he was dead weight in my life and career. It was too bad we wasted a year and a half on each other.

Jonathan called while I was still driving. I picked up the phone and answered his questions simply, with no cadence or energy in my voice. "About an hour away. Yes, I'm fine. I have the address."

He ended the call by saying, "I can't wait to see you, baby!" and the words screeched in my ears and made my mouth dry. I hated him. I felt played, betrayed, and stupid. But I wasn't going to say anything on the phone. I needed to *see* his jerky face.

As I pulled up to the condo, I saw Jonathan and his friend Jen race down the outside cement stairs to greet me. I tried not to pull back too much from the obligatory kiss and hug and give myself away. We walked to Jen's apartment down a path surrounded by palm trees and hibiscuses in bloom, and I fought to control my urge to smash my suitcase over his head. I felt terrible having to meet this sweet friend Jen under these sour circumstances. The poor girl, she kept flashing me these big beaming smiles, but I had nothing to give her back. I knew the disdain was all over my face, my bottled-up fury slowly seeping out of my pores and perfuming the air. She probably thought I was a bit of a cold bitch, but she'd forgive me once she found out why I was acting so bizarre.

It was getting late and Jen was an early riser, so she bid us goodnight. I did not want to retreat to our air mattress room and start freaking out with abandon. I wanted it to be controlled and specific and effective. Jonathan closed the door behind us and asked innocently, "Are you okay? Did something happen on the way down?" It was enough to light my fuse. I burst into insults, starting with calling him a sexist pig, and moving on to a lousy misogynist who couldn't see past a girl's fucking vagina, and that he certainly didn't deserve me.

"What are you talking about?"

"I found your stupid list. You must have felt like a really big man writing that list," I seethed.

"What list?"

"Don't pretend to be an idiot."

"I'm serious, Ophira. I don't know what list you're talking about."

"Oh—there are others? Perfect. The list of all the fucking girls you've been with! I found it when I was transferring your stupid comic files."

I could see it dawn on him, and then he sank into a chair. Fuck. This was really happening. We were breaking up.

"No, that's not a list . . . well, it is a list, but I wrote it, like, a year ago, when we first met, because I wanted to do a comic strip for this sex anthology, and I was trying to organize my thoughts."

"Well, you have the thoughts of a misogynist pig. It's revolting how you think about your exes." I couldn't believe I was defending his exes. Also, I'd run out of words to describe a woman-hater, so I was recycling.

Jonathan exhaled hard. "I know exactly how that must have come across to you, but that's certainly not how I see you or women in general. It was for this story that I never wrote. How can you not know that about me? You know how I see you."

"Yeah. You see me as a 'comedienne.'"

"What's wrong with that?"

"No one uses that term! It's like 'spinster.'"

"Oh, sorry—I didn't know. I thought that was fine."

"It's not."

"Okay. I'm sorry. I love you. It was just a stupid list for a strip."

Even though I'd taught him the word *sorry*, it still felt meaningful to hear it.

"And for what it's worth, I never want to update that list," he said very softly.

Fuck. I wasn't moving to LA.

Slowly, I began to consider the idea that maybe I was wrong, or at least blew things way out of proportion. Maybe I wasn't blind to who Jonathan was. It was a little ridiculous to assume that he was some sort of psychological mastermind who could hide who he truly was from me for over a year. I stewed, crouched on the corner of the air mattress, trying to let my anger deflate, and finally permitted Jonathan to hug me. Then, much to my surprise, we had sex. Even though it was air mattress sex, it was some of the best sex we'd ever had, top-ten-list kind of sex. Take that, number twenty-two.

Jonathan read over his own list the next day and really didn't think it was that big of a deal, but we agreed to drop the conversation. On the flight home it crossed my mind that I should be happy there were fifty-four girls. Imagine if I were one of four. Chilling. It was time to stop wasting energy waiting for the other shoe to drop and have a little faith in what we had. I pulled out my phone and deleted a couple of numbers.

CHAPTER 19

VANILLA MISTRESS

I was experiencing all kinds of unfamiliar sensations, like waking up and thinking, *Is it possible that I love this guy more than I did yesterday?* It was a gigantic step up from, "Where the hell is my other boot?" Don't get too excited—my feelings of accelerating adoration for Jonathan would then plateau for a solid week—but still, I didn't know that I could feel like that at all. When I asked Jonathan about seeing my scar every day, he said, "You know what? I don't even see it anymore. I just see you." Still, my neurosis could not be subdued. I was plagued by a brand-new variety of inner turmoil: that I'd never have another wild adventure again. There was no denying that I was where I wanted to be. If only it didn't feel so itchy and prickly on my skin. I missed throwing myself into the night, open to whatever basement it would take me to. But I'm not an idiot; I knew sabotaging a good thing for the sake of chasing a thrill wasn't the answer. I needed to jam that into my head—everything comes with a trade-off.

Now I was headlining at a few clubs, performing in a new storytelling scene, and doing some readings. After one of these shows, where I told the tale of losing my virginity and a bet on the same night, I received an e-mail from an editor at a glossy woman's magazine aimed at twenty-five- to thirty-five-year-olds, a demographic I was on the cusp of leaving. This editor enjoyed my comedy and thought I'd be a great fit for their audience. She wanted to know if I had an idea for a stunt piece. It was exactly what I was looking for to fill the adventure void. Finally, I could justify some ridiculous, bizarre thing I'd always wanted to do with the perfect excuse: It was a job. I would be like Hunter S. Thompson, a *Gonzo* journalist, a writer in the field. I would actually use my anthropology degree! My entire life made sense in that one moment.

Then I reread her e-mail.

She wasn't looking for any stunt piece; she wanted a *sex* stunt piece.

What does that even mean? After intercourse you stick your landing?

My chin receded into my head as I digested the premises of past articles she sent as examples: a woman who'd used a make-a-dildo-of-your-boyfriend's-penis kit, another who'd won an orgasm contest, a third who'd worn a remote-control vibrator in her underwear for a day.

The dick-molding kit seemed too arts-and-craftsy for my taste; the remote-control vibrator sounded plain annoying—who'd want to endure an entire day shifting around, stifling gasps, and silently screaming, "Slower and slightly to the left, goddammit!"; and the orgasm contest was beyond my scope of understanding. I couldn't think of anything less titillating than masturbating for the sake of sport in front of a bunch of random people drinking boxed wine out of dirty glasses.

Then I remembered Mistress Amy.

When I first moved to New York, the majority of my gigs were free shows at little bars where the people in the crowd didn't know a comedy show was about to ruin their evening, a process I called "terrorist stand-up." One night after a seven-minute set at some Irish pub, I was told that a couple was waiting to speak to me. I was immediately filled with delusional hope. *They must be casting directors! They recognize my potential and want to polish me into a star.* It was more likely they were from Immigration and Naturalization Services, there to drag me back up north.

But realistically, not even the INS could have found this show.

I peered outside and saw this odd couple loitering near a wrought-iron banister—odd in the sense that they were both so intensely good-looking. We shook hands awkwardly. I couldn't stop examining their faces, trying to find a flaw. She was a classic, stunning blonde with a cultivated dark edge, like a delicate flower that slices your nose when you sniff it. Her boyfriend sported a rough-and-tumble biker look, contrasted by a gentleness in his eyes that said, "I love kitties." They didn't immediately praise my performance, but did insist on taking me for a drink.

Without giving it a second thought, I accepted. For one, it was the polite thing to do. For another, I didn't have enough money to buy

244 ~ SCREW EVERYONE

myself a drink and really wanted one. I followed them to a nondescript bar, one of those places that changes its name and management so often that people refer to it as "Grand Opening."

Within minutes of sipping my Shiraz, I spilled my soul to these strangers. I whined about my struggle to get situated in the city and how the only job I could find was in phone sales. I was so beaten down by people's rudeness, I'd begun engaging in something I termed "reverse telemarketing." I'd call someone, and after they said "Hello," I'd yell, "Not interested! Go fuck yourself," and hang up. I'd barely started the game and was already losing. The couple nodded and smiled patiently.

As it turns out, there's no such thing as a free Shiraz.

The blonde, Amy, complimented my stage presence. It made her think that maybe I'd consider dabbling in her line of work. They were currently hiring.

Great, another sales job, I thought. *What would it be this time? A fancy jewelry store? A catering outfit? Receptionist at her modeling agency?*

No. She worked at a private club. As a dominatrix.

Of course she did.

My face blanched. The whole thing had to be a joke. I wasn't the type. I was more the girl-next-door's even nicer friend who'd just moved here from Canada. My entire life had been spent happily agreeing to take care of neighbors' cats or water their African violets. Sure, occasionally they'd return to new cats and different plants, but they never had to question what I was up to in their basement.

Still, the offer gave me a bit of perspective. A performance has to be a certain kind of painful if someone offers you an S&M–related

job after seeing it. But she was referring to my control of the audience, so that was something. And it wasn't the first time someone assumed that with my dark hair, bangs, red lipstick, and desire to work in various male-dominated fields, I must be into punishment on some level, and unconventional in the sack. I'd tried, but so far I was still kinkless.

However, dollar signs challenged me to think differently. The more *Mistress* Amy talked about her job, the more it sounded safe, relatively easy, and perfectly reasonable, which showed how desperate I was to rationalize it. It involved a lot more psychological punishment and role-playing than anything approximating actual sex. She was always fully clothed, the guys weren't allowed to touch her, and when I asked her if they ever *finish* during the session, she casually nodded, but added that you can make them clean it up—they'll do anything to please you. For all this she made between four and seven thousand dollars a month, depending on the season. Christmas must be nuts. Those numbers certainly impressed me. She even offered to show me the ropes—*and whips and chains and straps*—herself.

Another Shiraz arrived.

Mistress Amy and her biker boy-toy whispered to each other about my body type and pointed at my torso. Without warning she approached like a doctor and cupped her hands around my chest. She squished my boobs together and glanced at her boyfriend. "They're small," she noted, "but with the right corset, I think it could work."

Embarrassed and slightly titillated, I thought, *This is what a submissive must feel like.* There was something undeniably hot about a gorgeous woman and her manly boyfriend suggesting you might be in their club. In "the right corset," that is.

Flashdance sequences swirled through my head. Next I'll be telling a Ralph Fiennes look-alike that he's a piece of shit, whipping a Wall Street executive in a light-gray suit, and then counting hundred dollar bills.

Back in my disheveled sublet, I dropped my jacket and keys and eyed myself in the mirror. I tried one dangerous-yet-sultry look but saw a goofy-faced brunette wince back at me. *Whatever.* I just needed practice. I knew I'd be good at it and even suspected that this might be the beginning of something life altering. The dual life, the secret identity, the power, the costuming, the MONEY. It all appealed to me. How would I explain my fat wallet to my family at Passover? They'd never buy that it came from telling jokes. It would be a good problem to have. Everyone wants to be naturally gifted at something; they just need a mentor to point them in the right direction.

Since my own rational inner voice had laryngitis, I collect-called my recent ex at the time, Henry. He was still my voice of reason. We were hanging on to each other, operating under the false impression that we could break up, weather the crisis of my move, and immediately segue smoothly into friendship. That was the kind of torture with which I was familiar.

Appropriately, Henry quickly burst my leather-hooded bubble.

"Really? You're going to work in the fetish sex trade? That's what you moved to New York City to do?" he scolded. "What is wrong with you?"

He had a point. I didn't get into stand-up comedy to perform at a fetish club, and it was a little extreme to resort to a job in the sex trade after struggling for only a couple of months. Training as a dominatrix was a deep detour from headlining at the Chuckle Hut. I was so taken by that striking couple. Mistress Amy was good. I almost took her up on her offer just because I wanted to please her.

I'D LONG LOST her business card, but I could still go out and try it on my own—right? The timing was ideal. It could be my last chance to do something eyebrow-raising in the sex arena. I could tie up some loose ends, end the debate as to whether or not this was my secret calling as a natural control freak with an edgy bob, and gather a few extra tricks for down the road when sex with Jonathan needed to be freshened up. So I wrote the editor that I'd like to train as a dominatrix and then go to an event or party to try out my new skills.

As soon as I hit *Send* I second-guessed myself. My pitch was so *not* a fit for this glossy magazine's audience. I pictured an office where young manicured girls with fixed noses sat in pastel-colored cubicles, sipping soy chai lattes. They'd want more of a "How I Got Pregnant on a Pilates Reformer" article, or "Why Men Don't Make Passes at Girls with No Asses." But to my surprise and chagrin, I received a reply almost instantly from the editor saying she *loved*—with fifteen exclamation points—the idea and would arrange for a clothing budget.

I was slightly concerned about Jonathan's reaction to the feat at hand. The poor guy deserved to have a nice girlfriend, but instead he got me. First he had to deal with the ups and downs that came with dating a performer, and now I was asking his consent to check out the world of sadomasochism. You could say I kept him on his toes.

When I told him about the stunt piece, his first question was, "How much are they going to pay you?" This was a testament to where we were at in our relationship. If I'd told him about this on date two, he would have wanted to kill any guy I laid my hands on or been curious and aroused as to what his fringe benefits might be. Now it was all about what expensive dinner we could treat ourselves to at the end of the exercise.

I walked into Trash and Vaudeville on St. Marks Place and bought a black vinyl tank top with gigantic metal safety pins up the front, and a black pencil skirt with zippers up the front and back and latches covering the sides. I already owned fishnets and black patent stilettos. What girl doesn't? There was a latex dress I had my eye on, but it was vanity, not prudishness, that stopped me from purchasing it. Seeing your body draped in rubber is like seeing your face in HD. Until I'd completed ten weeks with a trainer and undergone a body cleanse, that outfit would dominate *me*.

When I got home I modeled the ensemble for Jonathan. He laughed, claiming that somehow I'd purchased the most sophisticated domme get-up out there.

Next I googled workshops and events, and enrolled in a class called "Intro to Scene Etiquette for Novices." It sounded very New School. The workshop took place in a room that resembled a run-down dance rehearsal studio. The other attendees looked like the same people I'd meet at a book launch or wine tasting: girls with dyed black hair and black cat-eye glasses, men with full arm tattoos wearing sixty-dollar distressed T-shirts, a couple of bearded guys smelling of Asperger's, and one frazzled woman struggling with her nylons, who clearly rushed there straight from work.

It started much like an improv class would: We placed chairs in a circle and went around stating our names and identifying whether we were a dominant, a submissive, or weren't sure. There was no way I could use my own name, so I went with "Jane" for the harshest contrast. A woman in a powder-blue button-down shirt chose to pass. Sizing her up, I was pretty sure she was also a journalist—a better one, as it never occurred to me to pass.

After a flogging demonstration, where the instructor hit the back of a chair with a cat o' nine tail and told us we would be "blown away" by the amount of people who flail inaccurately, we were given an explanation of the rules and safe words, told why service slaves are superior to wives, and asked to restack our chairs and sign the mailing list on our way out. I left with the sense that I didn't understand what I was getting into and that I should get Jonathan a service slave for his birthday.

I picked Saturday night to try out my skills, since the article was due on Monday and dungeons are closed on Sundays in observance of god knows what. Back on Google, I whittled down my choices to two events: "Slave to Lust" or "OTK Spanking Party." "Slave to Lust" sounded like a Prince album, so I was naturally drawn to it. The description was also hard to beat: "twenty-five hundred square feet of intimate play space with the only private roof deck overlooking the New York City skyline."

I loved the idea of a fetish party with a view. The mere vision of a leather-hooded man opening his mouth zipper to say, "Look, Mistress! It's the Chrysler Building!" would be worth every penny. However, it cost sixty dollars for single males, but was free for single females, which meant I'd be the only woman there. Then I noticed the address was in Long Island. No thanks.

The OTK Spanking Party at Paddles cost thirty-five dollars for men and five dollars for women. It was nice that they were letting the ladies chip in a little. OTK stood for "Over The Knee." Delightful! The club was described as a "five-thousand-square-foot, state-of-the-art location with twenty years of safe, clean, S&M fun." Spanking, paddling, hairbrushes, rulers, wooden spoons, straps, and canes were encouraged, but it was noted that patrons should check whips, chains, and gags at the door until 10:00 PM.

Maybe I should get there at noon.

What was with the square-footage obsession in the ads? Was there a bondage Olympics that I was unaware of, with the 200-meter breast-clamp stroke and 500-meter dog-leash walk? Actually, that sounded perfectly plausible.

I decided to check out OTK, which also included a preparty "munch." It sounded vaguely lesbianesque, but *munch* is a term used to describe an outing where a bunch of S&M and bondage enthusiasts meet at a vanilla place, in this case, a diner. I stuffed the outfit in my bag, along with a bottle of Purell, and pulled out the fliers for my upcoming comedy shows.

The group wasn't hard to spot. For one, they were sitting in the very back of the restaurant, beyond the dessert carousel and a dusty Christmas tree. Second, they were too mismatched to be a group of friends. They looked like a basket of single socks. I gave them the name Lindsay—I was done with Jane—and the group warmly welcomed me. I sipped screw-top chardonnay and watched them eat Denver omelets. Half the attendees had recently returned from a spanking convention, appropriately called "Smack," held at a Hilton Garden Inn in Arizona. Harold, who looked like a sleazy version of Einstein with crazy, frizzy white hair and a faded Planet Hollywood sweatshirt, said that being there for three days was like a dream come true.

I was a tad distracted, scanning the table for the young hot guys. Where were they? These people seemed nice enough, but I was not into doing anything kinky with them. It'd be like crashing your parents' friend's key party.

A distinguished-looking lawyer-type sat down beside me after pushing in the chair of his Asian girlfriend. He introduced himself as Kenneth and his girlfriend as Tanya. For some reason, I thought these were the people I could joke around with, so I leaned in and said, "Pretty crazy group, right?"

Instead of responding with a smirk and a nod, Kenneth looked at me in a way that triggered creepy tingles down my spine.

"Are you a top or a bottom? A domme or a sub?"

That was when it hit me: S&M is not funny. It's serious.

"*Um . . .* domme?" I'd never felt more sub.

Ken seemed unfazed by my tentative answer and continued with his interview. "Have you ever topped a woman before?"

"*Uh,* yeah, sure—who hasn't?" What the fuck was coming out of my mouth?

"Good. Because I could use some help with her later." Tanya giggled childishly behind an invisible fan of stereotypical servitude.

I turned my attention to Dorothy, a fifty-year-old woman who reminded me of my elementary school lunch-lady. Trying to get my article back on track, I asked, "*Um,* does everyone change out of their street clothes before we head to the club?"

"Oh no, dear, most people wear what they already have on."

Even the Planet Hollywood sweatshirt? I was expecting eye candy: Girls dressed up in velvet gowns and nurse's outfits, guys resembling Roman gladiators or mad scientists. Instead, it was a bunch of middle-aged folks dressed by Target. Dorothy pointed to a large man who looked like he worked at *The Sopranos* theme park. "Except for him. Wait until you see what he changes into!"

We were about to walk to the club when my friend David texted that he was at a nearby bar. I was starving to talk to someone who knew my real name. I asked Dorothy if she could give me the address of the club, and I'd catch up with them a little later. There was no real address. I was told to look for a door painted black at one end of a parking lot on 27th Street. The Nancy Drew in me smiled.

Peeling off from the group, I practically sprinted to the gay dive bar where David was drinking, and justified my own presence by thinking, *It's cool—I'm just nervous and could use a couple of drinks to loosen up.* I didn't want to seem like an irresponsible journalist, so I ordered a double Grey Goose because vodka doesn't make your breath smell.

Then I ordered another.

And another.

As the liquor took hold, I made the mistake of admitting to David's friends that I was going to an S&M club later, and my outfit was stashed in my bag. Of course they demanded that I put it on for them.

I was plastered drunk in the cubicle bathroom, literally bouncing off the walls of the stall while pulling on my fishnets. When I finally emerged in my vinyl outfit and high heels, it was like I was hitting a red carpet. Everyone started screaming and catcalling. Cell phone cameras were flashing, strobe lights were flickering, gay guys were touching me . . . I felt like Cher, Christina, and Lady Gaga all at once. My heels were about as high as my blood alcohol level, and I could barely manage either. But it was getting late and I had to get to the club. Noticing my friend David was looking rather dapper in his pinstripe denims, I grabbed him by his red tie and slurred in his ear, "You have no choice. You're coming to a sex club with me right now!"

He nonchalantly replied, "Ah . . . okay. Let me say 'bye to a few people."

As we sped downtown in a cab, I took stock of what I was doing. Did I have any boundaries tonight? How much of this was for the article? I made the decision right there and then that, whatever happens in the dungeon stays buried in the dungeon. This was my one night to let loose with abandon and do whatever I wanted. I wouldn't hold back.

The small painted-black entrance at the far end of the parking lot was easy to spot, although I never would have noticed it otherwise. We opened the unmarked metal door and passed through a curtain of plastic vinyl strips, like giant hanging flypaper, and started our descent four flights down.

I was getting a contact high of excitement off David as he practically skipped down the stairs with glee. We drew back a heavy maroon curtain, and there we were: midnight on a Saturday in New York City's premier S&M club! And the place was . . . empty. There were about seven people wandering around bored in leashes. This did not bode well for my one night of freedom. Maybe there was a secret room with a bunch of people somewhere else? I paid for both our cover charges but was too embarrassed to ask for a receipt for my expense report.

The place was massive, like a two-story Sam's Club, but underground. We walked down a hallway filled with torture equipment: a medical bench, a dog cage, a spanking bench, and lots of other apparatuses that resembled gym equipment, the kind that could be wiped down easily. Finally, I saw something I could relate to: the bar, adorably called the Whips and Licks Café.

Here I discovered something more torturous than the most extreme S&M scene: They didn't serve alcohol—only soda, water, and coffee. While I couldn't imagine spending a second there sober, most of the patrons couldn't imagine using anything that might numb the pain. It wouldn't be practical or cost effective.

From the corner of my eye I spotted the *Sopranos* guy from the munch. He had definitely changed. He was wearing a turquoise baby-doll dress and white tights, ruffled socks, Mary Janes, and a curly wig. He reminded me of a doll that I had when I was a kid called Tiny Tears. It cried real tears. Tiny Tears had a twin brother called Timmy

Tears. If you dressed Timmy Tears in Tiny Tears's dress, added forty years and a hundred pounds, you'd get this guy, and I was pretty sure he wanted to cry.

I turned to share my joke with David, but instead almost kicked a middle-aged shirtless man with a shaved head on all fours at my feet. In a loud whisper he said, "I am at your service, Mistress, if you so wish."

I didn't know what to say. But I had to say something. I didn't want to disappoint the man, but I wasn't ready yet. It was all coming at me too fast.

But he was waiting. With all my inner-domme strength, I responded in a low register, "Not now! Maybe later!"

"Thank you, Mistress," he mumbled, and scuttled away, leaving me shaking in my stilettos. My inner monologue resumed, *Drink your root beer. You're going to be great at this.*

David was doing his own exploring and giddily waved to me from the second level, a red-carpeted room with a hangman structure, a star with shackles, and the stocks. David was the type of gay man who loved Renaissance fairs, and he begged me to help him get into the stocks. His giggling and unabashed enthusiasm relaxed me. Why was I taking all of this so seriously? I lifted up the heavy top part so he could get in, then lowered it down. His head and hands dropped out of the wooden holes. He looked ridiculous.

"Okay, now spank me!" he said with a grin.

I thought it was sort of funny, so I smacked him lightly over his jeans with my hand, and out of nowhere a small crowd gathered to watch.

Worried, I whispered, "David, get into character. It's showtime!"

I started spanking him harder for the benefit of my audience, shouting, "It's for your own good! You should learn to take your punishment with a smile! Yeah! You are very bad!" and then muttered under my breath, "Are you okay?" David gave me a thumbs-up.

I felt a cold hand on my shoulder and spun around to find a mustached man in black leather. He handed me a wooden ruler and introduced himself as Bill. He was one of the owners and wanted to welcome me and offer some pointers. He instructed me to whack the ruler around on David's butt. As soon as I did, an image appeared in my head: Now I was an evil schoolteacher and David was a bad speller!

Bill stood by and threw out instructions. "Aim more for the bottom, fleshy area. Now alternate hitting with rubbing in small circles. Good! Good! Try paddling his inner thighs. Look at that! You're a natural!"

I was concentrating so hard on being Bill's star pupil that I didn't notice that I was beating the shit out of David, until I heard " . . . soy chai latte . . . *soy chai latte!* SOY CHAI LATTE!"

That was our safe word.

I helped David out of the stocks. He genuinely seemed pleased, but I had no time to register what had just happened as men lined up to get punished. It was time to put in my hours.

I started with the bald man who approached me earlier. After all, he was first.

Bill handed me a leather riding crop—very stylish. I started on baldy and tried to talk the talk but could only come up with uninspired dialogue. "You're bad! So bad! You know it!" I was basically reciting Michael Jackson lyrics, so I tried to switch it up. "Tell me. Why are you bad? Huh? Why are you bad? Yeah. Tell me! Why are you bad?"

And then he answered. "Because I've been thinking of younger and younger girls all the time."

There was a hush in the dungeon.

Note to self: Never, ever, ever, *ever* ask someone why they are bad. Just assume while we were in the dungeon, we're *all* bad.

Part of me wanted to turn to the crowd like an expert showman and say, "It's okay, everyone! I know this guy admitted to being a latent pedophile, but I'm going to smack him a few more times, because that's why we're here, right? And then we can all go home and hope for the best. Is there a therapist in the house? No, for me."

But he sensed my hesitation and whispered, "That's enough," and like a bad dog crawled away.

My feet hurt, and I didn't feel sexy. I felt desired but in a way that didn't turn me on. I liked the theater of it but had no emotional connection to administering punishment. The majority of the people there—at least six out of the seven—had a deep, unflinching desire they needed to fulfill, an itch to be scratched. I wasn't sure if I was too fucked-up or not fucked-up enough to get it. Or just fucked-up enough to question the whole domme/sub thing, which is a problem only found in the first world.

Bill brought me back to the sub reality by introducing me to a guy who wanted to be trampled. He was in his forties and possibly Jewish. Hadn't our people suffered enough? Apparently not. I wanted to go home, but everyone was so eager to play with me that I felt bad and didn't want to let them down. I was the most popular girl in the dungeon. And coincidentally, the only one.

Bill hoisted me on top of this poor guy, and he screamed in pain that my heels were too intense. He asked politely if I could take off my shoes. I wanted to check in with Bill on the rules—is he allowed to tell me what to do?—but he was busy strapping someone to a bench, so I tossed off my heels and hopped on the stranger's chest with my fishnetted feet. I watched pain creep onto his face, like a kaleido-scope turning. His eyes bulged out of their sockets, and his expression became devilish, dark, and almost beastly. A carnal voice from within him suddenly screamed, "Mercy!"

I jumped off, and his normal expression returned. He thanked me and asked if I'd like another root beer. I was completely envious. It must be so nice to know specifically what you like in life.

A guy named Rich, wearing a dog collar and black yoga pants, reminded me he was next. While taking off his pants, he told me he could really take pain. Bill searched through his bag, and with a glint in his eye, handed me an electric bug zapper. It looked like a small squash racket with fine silver mesh, and when I tested it by lightly touching it to my palm, a shivering zap that both stung and burned ran through my arms and legs.

Rich said he could take five of them. With every touch, his body flinched and crumbled. On the fourth swing, I missed his butt com-pletely and instead tagged his defenseless balls.

Horrified, I cried out, "Oh my god, I'm so sorry! Are you okay?"

Then I turned a shade of red slightly brighter than his ass and instinctively embraced his fallen body in an awkward spoon-like hug.

Rich turned around and gave me a puzzled look and then laughed. It was clear he was laughing at me. Bill joined in, and between giggles, pulled me off the ground, put his arm around me, and proclaimed that I was the "cheeriest domme" he'd ever met. Not exactly the quality you look for in a top.

I was totally disappointed. I'd hoped to have a sort of epiphany; understand my own sexual appetite in a deeper, more profound way; and get it on. Instead, it reinforced that I was nice—a people pleaser who was not at all dangerous—and painfully middle-class. If anything, *I* was the submissive. I'd let everyone tell me what to do: Bill, the pedophile, Jewey McCrazy Eyes, Richie Balls, even the editor at the magazine. The only person who was my approximate equal throughout the whole process was Jonathan, who'd texted me, *How's it going Mistress O? Ha!*

The whole scene was so cut-and-dry. Where was the flirtation? The sushi rolls? The torture in not being sure if you can close the deal? But the men didn't seem to care that I was going through a mid-dominatrix crisis.

As I gathered up David to leave, Richie Balls and Jewey McCrazy Eyes called out, "Thank you, Mistress! Thank you, Mistress! Please come back, Mistress."

One thing was certain: A cheery mistress was better than no mistress at all. As I shook Bill's hand and thanked him for his instruction, one last hopeful notion ran through my head: I wondered if any of these guys would like to come to a comedy show. But I guess we weren't exactly exchanging business cards here.

Back at our apartment, Jonathan was fast asleep and the television was rolling credits for *The Matrix Revolutions*. My outfit must have inspired him. I woke him and asked if he had a deep, burning desire to be spanked, flogged, trampled, or otherwise humiliated. He sleepily responded, "God, no! Life's too hard! I like a strong massage though."

It made me smile.

I called my editor the next day to come clean. "Listen, I really tried, but it turns out I don't get it. I was terrible at the whole thing. I got an intense triceps workout, but I don't think I'll be bringing any of the principles I learned in S&M into my own relationship."

The editor seemed unmoved. "Okay—so you're a Vanilla Mistress."

I laughed, but was confused by her use of words. "A what?"

"A Vanilla Mistress. You know—like vanilla ice cream. Plain."

I wanted to correct her that no, the people in the dungeon were plain. They liked one thing and one thing only. I, on the other hand, was very complicated. Neopolitan-mixed-with-mint-in-a-chai-latte complicated.

"You're just not into the whole S&M thing. It's okay. We've had about seven writers pitch us this same article before, but no one seems to be able to actually write it. Keep the outfit though. It's on us."

I should have gone for the latex.

CHAPTER 20

KNOW WHEN TO
FOLD 'EM

The Peter Pan bus carrying me home from Lancaster, Pennsylvania, finally pulled into Port Authority Bus Station. I looked rumpled, felt beaten down, and had the sniffles. I don't care how on top of the world you are when boarding a bus; an hour into the trip you'll be braiding a noose out of your own hair. Added to this was my most recent injury: dying on stage in front of a room full of Christian lesbian alcoholics in recovery—which is a long way of saying, "Not my crowd."

The funniest thing about the whole gig was that I got booked to do it. They'd originally secured a prominent gay female comedian, but she canceled at the last minute, so in a panic the event organizer did some creative googling. With the combination of "queer," "comedy," and "female," she found that I'd once played a lesbian in an episode of *Queer as Folk* and figured that was enough to qualify me to entertain her crowd. I would think hiring someone who played a lesbian for ten minutes on TV would be the exact opposite of a person who would appeal to an audience of actual gay women. Her flawed logic only exposed how much pressure she was under to find a replacement fast. I, in turn, was desperate for any paying gig, so we were all good! I was sure I could handle the crowd.

Wrong.

The organizer also failed to mention the "in recovery" part over the phone and chose to deliver that information backstage, fifteen minutes before the show. At the time, my set list covered two major themes: drinking and dating. For this show, I had prepared by removing all the pronouns from my relationship jokes to make them sound more universal: "You know when you're on a first date and *that person* doesn't pick up the bill? And you think, do I still have to pleasure you orally?" But could I water down my alcohol-related material to make it work? "Who here still plays *cold medicine* games? Ever throw up after a long night of *Advil* and *St. John's wort* and think to yourself, 'Wow— that was expensive!'" I looked blankly at my notebook, hoping that if I stared at it long enough, the perfect jokes would materialize. If only I had a joke about field hockey or Melissa Etheridge.

Clenching my jaw, I gave myself a little pep talk. The upside of not working with a manager was that at least I didn't have to report back to anyone. The downside was that I had to talk myself into the game. The only way to make it through was to talk to the crowd. Hopefully, they'd be fun.

Wrong.

But in all fairness to this crowd, they were getting the raw deal. These women were not just saddled with religious guilt, they'd also relinquished the pleasures of drugs and alcohol. All they did was repent. Talk about Hell. And now they had to listen to me. Maybe empathy would get me through this gig.

It didn't help that the setup of the room was comedy death: A wireless microphone balanced on a stool in the middle of a massive dance floor with folding chairs set up along the edges, as if they were expecting a basketball team. That might not sound like a big deal, but trust me, the less a space looks like the standard comedy club—low lighting, low ceilings, and people crammed close together toward the front of the stage—the less successful the show is going to be. There I was, under a gigantic disco ball, stranded miles of parquet away from an audience of painfully sober women, with not one joke that they could relate to.

But there comes a point in every show that regardless of the shitty setup, the last-minute information, the mismatch of audience to performer, you have to put that all aside and get out there. It's too late. You have to take a step toward the stage, whisper to yourself whatever motivational saying works for you, and hope for the best. I always say, "They can all go fuck themselves." It's my mantra.

Since we were in the heart of Amish country, I told them that I wasn't "really a comedian—this was my Rumspringa." Then I made fun of the room, claiming that my contract states that I only perform in the "eye of the room," and that I felt a little like Diana Ross, alone under an enormous disco ball. "But don't worry, there ain't no dance floor large enough to contain my comedy." Then I sang a couple of bars of *Dancing with Myself* and moved gracelessly around the floor to an imaginary beat. They actually laughed at that. It was far from groundbreaking material—it wasn't even good—but it was goofy enough to create some warmth in the room and suspend harsh judgment for a few minutes. I foolishly believed that it might be possible to walk away unscathed.

But as the saying goes, three wrongs don't make a right.

I ran out of riffs about the weird room and the weird Amish, so I segued into a few jokes about my weird name. When I felt like I had them on my side, I defied orders and told my drinking games joke, justifying it by thinking they *used to* abuse substances, so at least they'd get it. Asking an audience in recovery to reminisce about the positive side of irresponsible *using* turned out to be a horrible idea, and the room went dead silent. I even watched a woman in the front row clutch the silver cross around her neck. My usual bad habit of scanning the crowd for the purposes of finding the person who was not enjoying me was far too easy; there were too many choices. Instead, my eyes darted around, trying to find anyone who didn't look annoyed. There was one woman excessively laughing and clapping, not at the right moments, but still behaving in a way that was appropriate to comedy. She wasn't angry but clearly mad-crazy, and she became my touchstone, the only thing that kept me going. I was able to muddle through the remaining thirty minutes because of her, which I whittled down to about seventeen. No one would complain that I got off stage too early.

The second it was over, I began to shake and quiver as the pent-up nerves overtook me. Failure nausea filled my gut, and I considered fleeing out the emergency exit, if only I could find it. Unfortunately they hadn't paid me yet, and I was hungry. Satisfying both of those needs meant returning to the ballroom and wading through the crowd to locate the event coordinator and the buffet.

I finger-combed my bangs, straightened my top, and told myself that regardless of what happened, my mother still loved me. Sort of. Everyone was mingling, sipping diet sodas, and swaying to Sheryl Crow's "All I Wanna Do." My usual way of dealing with a disaster-of-a-gig was to soothe the emotional aftermath with heavy drinking and light sex (see chapters 11–on), but I couldn't do that this time. It wasn't just because it was a dry event attended solely by lesbians—I'm sure if I had to, I could make that work. This self-imposed boundary had more to do with the new life I was building with Jonathan that I didn't want to fuck up because a room full of gay women booed me. At least not anymore.

The problem was that I had no idea what to do instead. It had all become such a habit, a reliable routine. I'd never worked out what I would use to replace it. I loved Jonathan, but thinking about his love did not relieve my angst. What was my emotional Nicorette? Food? Video games? Religion?

Everyone avoided making eye contact as I walked among them, except for that one woman, my big cheerleader in the crowd. She bee-lined in my direction. She was stunning in that au naturel kind of way, pulling off an adorable boyish haircut and cut-off jeans. I couldn't tell if I was attracted to her or just jealous.

"You were wonderful!" she bellowed in a voice that did not

match her exterior. Was it an Eastern European accent of some sort? I couldn't pinpoint its origin, only that she sounded a bit like my waxer. She extended her arms, inviting me in for a hug.

I agreed to it even though it felt patronizing. She gave me a hug that had meaning. Her body pressed right into mine, and her Pilates-trained arms gripped tightly around my back. It felt like a warm straightjacket. Was she coming on to me? Or just trying to make me feel better? I wrestled with the ethics of cheating and for a fleeting second thought, *It doesn't count if it's with a woman, right?* Even in my head it sounded pitiful, like an alcoholic justifying a glass of wine with dinner, knowing full well it would turn into hiding in the bathroom, guzzling Robitussin within days.

"Aw. That's very sweet. Thank you," I said, freeing myself from her embrace.

I looked right at her. She had fanatical eyes. They were espresso color and far too wide open, as if they were actually caffeinated. The expression on her face was somewhere in between scared-to-death and wildly excited. Why do I always attract the crazy ones?

"I'm Ophira," I said, extending my hand, which was ridiculous after body smushing.

"I already knew that! I'm Marcy. Your show was very, very funny, and I've seen Ellen DeGeneres. You made me laugh way more."

"Thank you," I said robotically.

Are these the kinds of things groupies tell guy comics? No wonder they have confidence to spare. Her compliment meant nothing to me because I knew it was nonsensical overexaggerated bullshit—and

I wasn't being coy. A ridiculous statement like that had more to do with Marcy not knowing what the hell to say, so she went with something fantastical. It's like looking at a child's finger painting and comparing it favorably to a Jackson Pollock. Either Marcy really needed to be liked by me, was totally deranged, or was actually one of Ellen DeGeneres's exes.

That being said, if she went with honesty and introduced herself by saying, "Hey, I could see you trying up there, but I guess it didn't work out this time," I would have punched her in the face.

"If you want another cuddle, you know where I am."

Was she offering to mercy fuck me? Comfort me? Or wax me? Women are complex, especially with a thick accent. The path of least resistance, for once, was to stick with my loyalty plan.

"It's really nice to meet you, Marcy. I know how these convention halls work, so I'm going to try to grab some food from the buffet before they take it away." Sure, *now* I sounded like a professional.

With my head hung low at the buffet, I shoveled some cold spaghetti onto a plate and disappeared up to my hotel room. I was too tired to wallow in the "what the fuck am I doing with my life?" debate, so I put the social suicide thoughts on hold, collapsed onto the bed, and watched a couple reruns of *Frasier*. Before I passed out, I called Jonathan. He tried to soothe me by promising that the gig probably wasn't as bad as I made it out to be; after all, I was my own worst critic. I tried to convince him that no, this was different. I wasn't exaggerating for the sake of drama, and this *was* really embarrassingly horrible, but he switched subjects to this new restaurant in our neighborhood that he wanted to check out when I got back. I was a little pissed that my pity party had ended so abruptly and told him that I was pretty sure I wouldn't be up for scoping out the new sushi joint in the hood right away. I wanted to get home, take a hot shower, and sleep for a week.

And then find a therapist. Who worked on a sliding scale.

ALL I COULD think about on the bus home was that much like Peter Pan, I had to grow up. I was worried though: Could my relationship carry me through the crappy times? Would it take the edge off a bad gig? How do other people do it? Was I going to have to learn about Reiki?

When I walked into our apartment hours later, I expected the familiar sight of Jonathan sitting on the sofa, crouched over his laptop, watching some documentary on TV. The first thing I noticed was that the place was clean. Suspiciously clean. Jonathan materialized from our yellow kitchen, gave me a big kiss, and said, "I made us some dinner!" What had happened while I was gone? Was he hiding something? Then again, the last time I thought I caught him surfing porn, it turned out to be a website called Mugglecast, a site for Harry Potter enthusiasts. No, when it came to Jonathan, my problem wasn't other women—it was other wizards. Besides, if he really was covering something up, he was doing a damn good job of it with the cleaning and the cooking. I applauded his time-management skills.

The foldout table was set, and Jonathan served up one of the two recipes he'd mastered: grilled salmon with grilled asparagus. The other one was grilled steak with grilled asparagus. I settled into my foldout chair (everything in a 350-square-foot apartment is foldout) and gulped down my dinner. As I mopped the salmon juice with the last asparagus spear on my plate, Jonathan casually took out a piece of red origami paper and started folding it. I know that sounds strange, but one of Jonathan's many hobbies is the Japanese art of paper folding. Not wood working, learning guitar, drinking whiskey, or even fetishizing Asian women—just the ancient Japanese art of paper folding. You can't be angry at someone for being into the Japanese art of paper folding. It's like yelling at someone for loving badminton. You have to let it go.

In a booming announcer voice, he started, "There are all these stories in Japanese folklore about a thousand cranes."

I looked around for a hidden studio audience, but, no, it was still just me.

I returned a crooked eyebrow, but he continued.

"Like if you fold a thousand cranes, it will bring you luck, or if you fold a thousand cranes, it will bring you health. But the one I like the best is, if you give the person you love a thousand cranes, your love will last forever."

He thumbed the final crease, checked that the wings flapped properly, and handed me the little red paper bird.

"This is number one thousand."

Time slowed as I accepted the crane. I looked at it confused. I knew something was up, because none of this was normal, but I didn't get it. Or I didn't let myself get it. Jonathan directed my eyes to the floor in front of the TV where the banker's box from the closet was now sitting.

"Why don't you open it up?"

Here we go. Here's where I see the severed head. *Please God, don't make her a blonde.*

I slowly lifted the lid like I was defusing a bomb.

Inside, I found 999 hand-folded paper cranes in a range of vibrant colors and sizes. It was breathtaking, one of the most amazing things I've ever seen. Also—a bit creepy. In the way that one ladybug is adorable, but a thousand is an infestation or an organized attack.

Jonathan explained that he'd been folding cranes for years as an exercise in patience. It helped with anxiety, and he loved the precision of it. As he continued to fold and collect them, he decided to attempt to reach a thousand. And when he did, the love of his life would be standing in front of him.

There I was, looking like a FEMA rescue and smelling like a bus. I couldn't believe he was talking about me. It was the most over-the-top amazing gesture I'd ever witnessed, only second to being told I was as funny as Ellen DeGeneres.

Had I found the most romantic man on the planet? Or was he obsessive-compulsive?

At least our doors would always be locked.

"Reach into the box," instructed Rain Man.

My hands dove in, and nestled among the cranes I felt a smaller box. *Holy shit.* I pulled it out slowly, letting the cranes fall away. I wanted to stop and take it all in, but the minute that little clamshell box was in front of my face, I could do nothing to stop myself from cracking it open.

Inside was a diamond ring.

Suddenly, I felt very drunk, even though I hadn't had a sip of anything.

Astonished, I looked up at Jonathan. I could feel blood circulating in my head.

He returned a nervous smile and asked, "Will you marry me?"

Marriage—the broken institution.

My single life flashed before my eyes. Sure, I'd traveled boldly from dance club to cocktail lounge to dive bar for years, getting myself in and out of subpar situations. But there were only so many walks, cab rides, and—heaven forbid—Metrocard swipes of shame one girl can endure. Finally someone was offering to make an honest woman out of me.

I was terrified.

I'd always maintained that the odds of a marriage lasting were less than 50 percent. Then again, the odds of making it in stand-up were far worse. Of anyone, I should know that 50 percent can also mean, you're gonna make it.

I'd certainly washed enough sheets, deleted enough phone numbers, and seen enough Garfields to have a pretty good idea of what I wanted. Or at the very least what I didn't want.

For a fleeting second I thought, *Shouldn't I count the cranes first? It looks like a thousand, but who knows? What if it's only 885?*

I gazed into Jonathan's innocent eyes—he didn't have one dog-fart joke in him.

I took a deep breath and stepped toward the next stage.

"Yes. Of course! Yes!"

We hugged and kissed, letting euphoria fill our little apartment. A unique feeling flooded through my body. I think it was joy.

My mother was right: You never really know someone until you live with them.

CHAPTER 21

UNBRIDLED

G etting married was one thing, but a wedding was a whole other ball of vanilla-scented wax. I never wanted a wedding even though I love going to them. I'm the first to hit my spoon to my glass to try to make the newlyweds kiss, I'll try to drink the open bar dry, and once the DJ starts, I'll dance like no one's watching. Who doesn't like a party? It's the ceremony I take issue with. On some level, I see it as equal to bridal capture, and I wanted no part in any ritual where I'd be given away like a possession. Fuck that.

What I *could* swallow was a simple civil service at city hall. It's possible that I would have thought differently if I were still in my twenties, a sorority sister, or believed in Jesus, but with none of that getting in the way, I was free to strip down the kidnapping ceremony to something that jibed with my philosophies. Convincing Jonathan would be another story. I hit him first with pragmatism, pointing out the major roadblock to throwing a wedding in New York: the expense.

Why would anyone short of a millionaire waste tens of thousands of dollars on a boring rental hall and dry chicken breast dinner? Jonathan agreed—about what a waste it would be to spend the money on such a pedestrian affair—but he wanted a wedding. More than that, he wanted a *wedding spectacular.* If cash flow and the laws of science were no issue, he would have us flown to the top of the Guggenheim on the back of a hippogriff while a gospel choir sang "Tradition" from *Fiddler on the Roof.* He'd wear a bespoke tuxedo, and I'd be dressed in a gown made of bubbles and sparkles. Jean-Michel Basquiat would be his best man, and Harvey Pekar would marry us. This would be followed by hot air balloon rides for all the guests, virtual reality games, and an IMAX screen playing *Once Upon a Time in the West* and *2001: A Space Odyssey.*

So we compromised—and got married at city hall.

Jonathan was concerned that the city hall idea would not go over with his family. His mother and father would be disappointed and at the very least demand to be there. Then his brother would have to join us, and then his cousins would feel left out, and within minutes the whole thing would turn into a stressful, messy gathering. On the other hand, there was no way that my family would bear the expense and fly out from Western Canada for a civil service.

So we settled on inviting *no one.*

We would elope in secret. Of course, the idea of a covert private wedding totally appealed to me: Could anything be more of a slap in the face to the ridiculous, overpriced wedding industry? Could anything be more fitting for a woman who'd gone against the grain of commitment her whole life? This was the only way to make sense of the madness and bring it back to what it should be: a simple practice required to obtain a piece of paper.

Frankly, I was surprised that Jonathan was cool with this idea. The guy can't keep a secret about a birthday gift, let alone a milestone. As he was a tireless romantic, getting married was precisely the kind of thing he'd want to shout through a bullhorn to the rest of the world. Facebook and Twitter were made for people like him. But he agreed—and I don't think it was just to shut me up. There must have been a part of him that was as apprehensive as I was, and thought, *If it fails, we can just get divorced and no one will know about that, either.* We'd both experienced feeling strongly about a life decision before, only to have it fall apart or require a change of heart. Neither of us had a tattoo . . . or even a gym membership.

Then again, how could one little piece of paper change us?

Or perhaps the better question was, how could it not?

We picked a day at the end of May and stuck to our plan not to tell a soul. Sharing this kind of major secret definitely had a thrill factor. We'd find ourselves talking about it rather sensibly—the times, the dates, the paperwork—and then catch each other's eye and exchange big dumb grins.

As I fell asleep the night before our city hall date, I found myself unexpectedly overwhelmed with emotion and no one to talk to about it outside of our bed. I distracted myself by fixating on the one thing that was within my control: What would I wear? I asked Jonathan how he planned on dressing, and he admitted that he hadn't thought about it. I was a little surprised but I kept it to myself and pushed forward. We decided that he should wear his old suit—not his worst suit, just his only suit. I dug through my closet, but nothing appealed to me, so I gave myself permission to take advantage of this once-in-a-lifetime (hopefully) opportunity and hit a couple of dress stores in the morning.

I walked into one of my favorite stores that I owned nothing from: Anthropologie. I loved the clothes there but considered them beyond my price point. I'd wander in occasionally, manhandle some pretty patterned fabric, take a look at the price tag, and scream, "You've got to be kidding!"

For a heartbeat I'd turn into my wartime-raised mother: "You'd think for that much money they could at least hem the dress! It only has two seams. What is it—a hundred dollars a seam?" Some clothing stores make you think, *You know what? I'm going to learn how to sew!*

But today was different. I didn't care how much the dress cost or how carelessly it was made. I was buying it.

Before long, I was twirling in front of a mirror in a flowery, cream-colored, A-line dress that fit me *almost* perfectly. It was delicate and pretty and horrifically overpriced, just like most wedding dresses.

I took it up to the cashier, who, like a good shop girl, smoothed it between tissue paper and commended my choice. "Oh my god! I love this dress. It's one of my favorite things in the whole store right now."

She baited me. I couldn't help myself. I had to tell her why I was buying it, just to see her reaction.

I leaned in toward her. "Really? Because I'm getting married in it in a couple of hours."

The blood drained from her face. She couldn't find her next

words. This was pages beyond what it said in the customer satisfaction training handbook. But I could see she felt scandalized, as if my being so cavalier about the most important day of my life tarnished her own bridal dreams. By purchasing that dress, I was letting down all young, beautiful women the world over. If everyone acted like me, there would be no weddings. There would be no tulle veils or tiny tiaras. After years of imagining, planning, and leafing through bridal magazines, she was suddenly faced with a marriage anarchist.

I could see her mind working, trying to make sense of this bridal princess of darkness who was despoiling her Vera Wang wedding dreams.

Finally, with a tight smile she said, "Well, it's not your first marriage, right?"

Wow.

"Yes, it's my first," I said self-righteously, savoring every minute of her discomfort while pocketing my credit card.

As I left the store, she yelped, "Well . . . you got a great deal on a wedding dress!" Positive yet disapproving. It was almost like having an actual bridesmaid.

THE PLAN WAS that Jonathan would leave work at lunchtime, and we would meet on the subway platform for the Downtown N at 23rd Street at 1:15 PM. At the very last minute, I ran into the DSW and bought a pair of gold Steve Madden wedges, changed into my outfit in the DSW staff bathroom (thanks to a broken lock), and hit that grimy platform at 1:10 PM, ready to get hitched with five minutes to spare. I was smiling. This was fun! It felt like I was the lead in an action movie, with a secondary romantic storyline. *Run, Ophira, Run.*

And I knew that I didn't doubt my choices at all. I was staying in New York and I was staying with Jonathan. Wow. There really was a first time for everything.

Trains whizzed by; the usual variety of hurried New Yorkers and spastic tourists got off and on. I watched and I waited. It was 1:15. Then it was 1:20. We all know it's impossible to time things perfectly when you're dealing with the New York subway, but then it was 1:30. My jaw clenched, and my eyebrows furrowed. What the hell was the holdup? At 1:35, I was still standing there alone, shifting my balance from one foot to the next because my toes were squished into the new gold Steve Madden sandals, adding injury to insult. As subway after subway shot by, I felt more and more stupid in my frivolous flowered sundress.

At 1:40, I yelled at God. "Really? This is how the story of my life goes? I finally give in and decide to get married, and the world conspires against me? You're just going to go ahead and let me get stood up on my wedding day on a dirty cement subway platform? That's what I deserve? I can't even be dumped above ground?"

As I was about to give in and trudge up the stairs to confirm that there wasn't a zombie apocalypse, I saw Jonathan race down, running like he was escaping from a burning house, sweating profusely, with a face full of remorse.

"Where the hell were you?" I yelled. Those were my first words to him on our wedding day.

"I don't know. Somehow I wasn't looking and I got on the express train by accident . . . and I figured it out too late. I saw you on the platform as we went by, and I was waving my arms, but I guess you couldn't see me."

No, I didn't see anyone beckoning from the hundred-mile-an-hour subway car shouting, "Ophira! I'm here! No, no, no, no, no!"

It was an uncharacteristic mistake for a native New Yorker to make. Maybe he was suffering from subconscious cold feet that the extra ten minutes on the express train somehow subdued? We got on the next train in silence. I was still angry, slow to recover from what could have been the biggest emotional disaster of my life. When Jonathan put his sweaty arm around me, I brushed it off.

"I need a minute," I barked. Say what you will, but I knew I looked sexy fuming in that dress. Worth every penny.

Getting married at city hall was about as romantic as getting married at the DMV. Even though the little wooden sign read CHAPEL, it felt like a generic government office, void of atmosphere and ambience. We stood in a long line with drunk college kids in front of us, and dubious green-card relationships behind us. Nothing in the Big Apple comes without a long line.

With fifteen minutes before closing time, we made it into the chapel, a bland room with a chipped brown desk, and stood between the American flag and the New York state flag. Our justice of the peace glanced over the top of her *New York Post*. Jonathan, with a quiver in his voice, told her that we didn't have our wedding rings yet, so she could skip that part. She nodded and without warning commenced her thirty-second state-approved civil nuptial speech. It was fast paced, with no variation or cadence to illustrate significance. She barely left enough space for us to throw in our "I dos." If we replayed the recording for quality assurance, I think we'd find out that Jonathan and I exchanged "I d-ahs."

Then we heard her say, "Please take her left hand and place the ring on it."

We both looked at her, unimpressed. Seriously? Could she not go off script for even one minute? Improvise for just a quick moment to make it seem vaguely personal? Sure, it was almost the end of her shift, but it was our FUCKING WEDDING DAY!

For someone so adamant about a simple ceremony, I was now pissed that people weren't making more of an occasion of things. If either of us had been more present, we probably would have interrupted her, but the whole experience was too overwhelming. Dazed, Jonathan took hold of my left hand, and when she recited, "Place the ring on the groom's hand," I grabbed his, like we were about to sashay out of there. While she finished up, flatly listing the different levels of government that now recognized us as legally joined, we stifled giggles, holding hands, braving it together. We waited for her to say something more to us—a congratulations, maybe? Instead, she looked at us and bellowed, "Next!"

With city hall behind us and joint tax returns ahead of us, we took a cab back to the Lower East Side to have a couple of glasses of prosecco at a little Italian place in our neighborhood. As we ordered a second round, a little dizzy from the magic bubbles, we blurted to our waiter, "We just got married, like an hour ago!"

With very little interest, he said, "Congratulations," and slapped down our check for the full amount.

Either he didn't understand us, didn't give a shit, or had seen it all before: *They come in all dressed up, and one glass of bubbly later claim they just got married to get free drinks.* Or maybe like the shop girl at Anthropologie, he couldn't fathom why anyone would choose to trade the intimacy and grandeur of their big day for a summer dress and a faux Italian café. It was hard to believe that even in such a diverse, nontraditional society like New York, people just couldn't wrap their heads around what we had done.

Or did this waiter look at me and think, *You don't look like the kind of girl who'd get married.*

There was something about the lack of formality, the skepticism from any layperson, and the undecorated rooms that worked in our favor. We compensated by caring more. In our little apartment we'd refer to each other as hubby or wife, and laugh: It was our little joke. There was no one to ask us when we were having babies, if we were going to move out to the suburbs, or how married life was going. It was just for us. And we kept it a secret for an entire year. If anything, we'd be arm and arm at a restaurant, and our friends would ask, "When are you two going to tie the knot already?" We'd look at each other and smile. "Probably next spring."

That year was the most romantic year of my life. A dear friend and fellow comic, Jo Caulfield, once said to me that the best thing about marriage is "you become closer in ways you can't imagine, and you have more independence in ways you can't imagine." When she first said this to me, I couldn't even conceptualize what she was talking about. But then I got it. With all the outside pressures removed, we blended our lives at our own pace.

A year later, on the exact same date, we called our parents and friends and told them that we had eloped at city hall. We were ready to face it all by then, their comments and criticisms. Our bond was tight, tested, and we'd passed. We'd gone from renewing leases with each other to buying, and it felt good.

The ongoing joke has become that when anyone asks us how long we've been married, our response is, "Five or six years, depending on whom you ask." They don't usually get it, but the truth is that after a few years no one but you remembers exactly how long it's been. Everyone has their own lives to think about, and it's that kind of necessary self-absorption we were counting on.

We ended up throwing not one but two small gatherings for our friends and family, one in Calgary, the other in New York, and sent out printed invitations with origami cranes affixed to them (I hand-folded about twenty-five of them). For a couple that didn't have a real wedding, we ended up having three marriage-related celebrations. Trading up from Anthropologie, I wore a long raw-silk dress made by my fashion designer friend, and Jonathan got himself two bespoke suits.

Only one friend commented that she thought I'd never tie the knot. But all my hard work had to amount to something. I had screwed my way through five cities and compiled an eclectic list of partners, the total number of which sounded impressive even to me. But you know what? It had paid off. I'd done it. I'd made an honest commitment. Don't get me wrong, I was still a weed, but a weed in choice conditions is a happy weed. I was content in my "first" marriage.

All I can say is, this one is sticking.

EPILOGUE

I was walking down Bleecker Street when my cell phone rang. I recognized the familiar Calgary area code, but not the number. I picked up, and it was my high school friend Cheryl. She'd recently moved back to Calgary and had received the invitation to our party, but by coincidence was planning on getting married on the same night. I joked that for once we'd finally both go through with something significant on the same night. She didn't quite follow. I brought up that weekend in Banff . . . the night I lost my virginity . . . the night she didn't . . . the air force pilots? The capers of Jasmin van Brunswick and Cheryl-Lynn . . . the night that shaped my life in many ways . . . remember? She said, "Oh yeah, I kind of recall that motel room. It had a weird smell."

It made me laugh. She didn't really remember. And to be fair, it wasn't as significant a trip for her as it was for me. I wasn't insulted or hurt in any way. It just goes to show that we are the stars of our own stories. Other people are supporting cast and recurring extras. Just ask the guy who "expanded my horizons," whatever his name was. Probably Dave.

ACKNOWLEDGMENTS

I want to thank my agent, Alia Hanna Habib, who saw me host a MothSlam and suspected there might be a book in me. This plainly wouldn't have happened if it wasn't for your support and direction; thank you for going above and beyond your call as an agent, time and time again.

I don't know how to begin to express my gratitude to The Moth, so I'll start with: Thank you to The Moth, especially Jenifer Hixson and Catherine Burns, for believing in me and providing the best stages on earth to tell stories.

Thank you to my editor, Krista Lyons—not only for your shaping and finessing skills, but also for putting up with my insane schedule and always making me feel like I was on track. You made the whole process so easy.

I asked for the meanest copy editor, but I got the best. A huge thanks to Merrik Bush-Pirkle, who transformed many of my awkward thoughts into sentences that sing. It was fun getting to know you through Track Changes.

I am fortunate to know a lot of stellar comics and writers, many of whom gave me superb advice, feedback, and even analysis on one or more of the seventy billion incarnations of this project over the years. Your friendship and brilliance are valued beyond a mere thank you in a book. I know I owe you one: Alison Shyer, Allison Castillo, Andy Christie, Bret Watson, Brian Preston, Charles Salzberg and the writers in the New York Writers summer workshop, Colin Macleod, Diana Spechler, Eric Pliner, James Ramsey, Lesley Grant, Lisa Kirchner, Michael Schellenberg, Ryan Brit, Stephen Vrattos, and, of course, Susan Prekel.

Also, a huge thanks to Avigail Eisenberg, my sister, for being there. Know I love you, but I don't really want you to read this book.

And a shout out to David Hodorowski, for agreeing to come to the dungeon.

I should probably thank everyone I screwed around with, although really, at this point, they should be thanking me.

ABOUT THE AUTHOR

Ophira Eisenberg is a stand-up comedian, writer, and host of NPR's new weekly trivia show, *Ask Me Another*. She has appeared on Comedy Central, VH1, E!, and TV Guide Network. She is also a regular host and storyteller with The Moth.

Ophira was born in Calgary, Alberta, Canada, and currently lives in Brooklyn, NY, with her husband, Jonathan, and their adopted Boston terrier, a former show dog named The International Delight Mocha.

SELECTED TITLES FROM SEAL PRESS

The Secret Sex Life of a Single Mom, by Delaine Moore. $17.00, 978-1-58005-386-0. The risqué story of a stay-at-home mom's boundary-pushing experimentations with sex—and resulting self-awakening—after a painful divorce.

What You Really Really Want: The Smart Girl's Shame-Free Guide to Sex and Safety, by Jaclyn Friedman. $17.00, 978-1-58005-344-0. An educational and interactive guide that gives young women the tools they need to decipher the modern world's confusing, hypersexualized landscape and define their own sexual identity.

Gawky: Tales of an Extra Long Awkward Phase, by Margot Leitman. $16.00, 978-1-58005-478-2. Tall girl Margot Leitman's memoir is a hilarious celebration of growing up gangly, a cathartic release of everything awkward girls are forced to endure, and a tribute to a youth that was larger than life.

Mind-Blowing Sex: A Woman's Guide, by Diana Cage. $16.00, 978-1-58005-389-1. An instructive, accessible sexual guide that will help women and their partners make their sex life more empowering, exciting, and enjoyable.

F 'em!: Goo Goo, Gaga, and Some Thoughts on Balls, by Jennifer Baumgardner. $17.00, 978-1-58005-360-0. A collection of essays—plus interviews with well-known feminists—by *Manifesta* coauthor Jennifer Baumgardner on everything from purity balls to Lady Gaga.

FIND SEAL PRESS ONLINE
www.SealPress.com
www.Facebook.com/SealPress
Twitter: @SealPress